Living and Dying Well

LIVING AND DYING WELL

A CATHOLIC PLAN FOR RESISTING
PHYSICIAN-ASSISTED KILLING

CHARLES CAMOSY

Our Sunday Visitor
Huntington, Indiana

Nihil Obstat
Msgr. Michael Heintz, Ph.D.
Censor Librorum

Imprimatur
Kevin C. Rhoades
Bishop of Fort Wayne–South Bend
April 8, 2025

The *Nihil Obstat* and *Imprimatur* are official declarations that a book is free from doctrinal or moral error. It is not implied that those who have granted the *Nihil Obstat* and *Imprimatur* agree with the contents, opinions, or statements expressed.

Scripture texts in this work are taken from the *New American Bible, revised edition* © 2010, 1991, 1986, 1970 Confraternity of Christian Doctrine, Washington, D.C., and are used by permission of the copyright owner. All Rights Reserved. No part of the *New American Bible* may be reproduced in any form without permission in writing from the copyright owner.

Excerpts from the English translation of the *Catechism of the Catholic Church* for use in the United States of America Copyright © 1994, United States Catholic Conference, Inc.—Libreria Editrice Vaticana. Used with Permission. English translation of the *Catechism of the Catholic Church: Modifications from the Editio Typica* copyright © 1997, United States Conference of Catholic Bishops—Libreria Editrice Vaticana.

Every reasonable effort has been made to determine copyright holders of excerpted materials and to secure permissions as needed. If any copyrighted materials have been inadvertently used in this work without proper credit being given in one form or another, please notify Our Sunday Visitor in writing so that future printings of this work may be corrected accordingly.

Copyright © 2025 by Charles Camosy
30 29 28 27 26 25   1 2 3 4 5 6 7 8 9

All rights reserved. With the exception of short excerpts for critical reviews, no part of this work may be reproduced or transmitted in any form or by any means whatsoever without permission from the publisher. For more information, visit: www.osv.com/permissions.

Our Sunday Visitor Publishing Division
Our Sunday Visitor, Inc.
200 Noll Plaza
Huntington, IN 46750
www.osv.com
1-800-348-2440

ISBN: 978-1-63966-284-5 (Inventory No. T2944)
1. RELIGION—Christianity—Catholic.
2. RELIGION—Christian Living—Death, Grief, Bereavement.
3. SOCIAL SCIENCE—Death and Dying.
eISBN: 978-1-63966-285-2
LCCN: 2025938026

Cover design: Tyler Ottinger
Interior design: Amanda Falk
Cover art: *Ars moriendi* (Art of Dying), World Digital Library

PRINTED IN THE UNITED STATES OF AMERICA

Contents

Introduction: On the Brink of What, Exactly?............ 6

Chapter One: What Physician-Assisted
  Killing Reveals About Our Culture 17

Chapter Two: The Example of Christ.................. 39

Chapter Three: Three Catholic Saints on Dying Well 51

Chapter Four: The Example of Catholic Monks and Friars 63

Chapter Five: Care Homes and Hospices Today 79

Chapter Six: Resisting Physician-Assisted
  Killing as Individuals 95

Chapter Seven: Resisting Physician-Assisted
  Killing as Families 111

Chapter Eight: Resisting Physician-Assisted
  Killing as Communities and Institutions 129

Appendix 1: Principles and Prayers.......... 147

Appendix 2: Practical Guidance.......... 151

Appendix 3: Responses to FAOs
  (Frequently Articulated Objections).......... 161

Notes.......... 167

INTRODUCTION

On the Brink of What, Exactly?

If you live in the contemporary consumerist Western world, it is very likely that you have a complex relationship with death. On the one hand, even if you are merely an occasional consumer of movies, video games, or streaming television, *death is thrust upon you from every direction*. Sometimes it is even explicitly celebrated. Perhaps you've encountered those who celebrate, for instance, the creation of Marvel films violent enough to earn an R rating or those who mock folks who worry about the mind-numbing and ever-more-graphic gore associated with first-person shooter video games.

On the other hand — in a remarkable paradox — *ours is at the same time a death-denying culture*. We push the firm and certain reality of dying and death out of our social consciousness. And we do this by pushing it out of physical spaces as well. Dead bodies, which two generations ago were regularly and prominently displayed in people's homes (often after dying at home) for visitation and viewing before burial, are today almost never seen outside funeral homes. And even that is becoming less and less common. Those who are dying are very often pushed outside mainstream culture — mostly to nursing homes and hospitals, where their final months and weeks are medicalized, technologized, and very often desperately lonely.

In a related story, the contemporary consumerist West presents us with another remarkable paradox when it comes to suicide. On the one hand, and mostly because of a significant remnant of Christian ethics that persists in our post-Christian culture, there are still stigma and presumption against it. We hang nets around bridges and seal windows in skyscrapers to discourage people from jumping. Antisuicide hotlines and links to other resources pop up if our Google search merely mentions the term *suicide*. Police and even random passersby will physically restrain someone (sometimes physically wrapping themselves around the at-risk person for hours[1]) to stop that person from ending his or her life. The de facto presumption is that the person's life is good.

Right alongside this presumption, however — especially as the consumerist West continues to secularize — we see something close to cheerleading for killing oneself when assisted by a physician. Brittany Maynard's 2014 quest to legally kill herself, and encourage others to fight for the right to kill themselves, was celebrated in many influential circles as heroic.[2] We will see much more about the promotion of physician-assisted killing in the next chapter, but consider that in both the Netherlands and Canada, the culture has been so deformed by the practice that many now support it for people who have decided that they have a "completed life." Also gone in many circles is any sense that human life is an end in itself that is good for its own sake. As a result of this loss, questions such as the following are now being asked rather openly: "Why do we keep severely mentally disabled people alive, other than the fact that they're human?"[3]

This paradox-filled tension is playing out right now in the consumerist West in ways that are quite dramatic. Indeed, it is fair to say we are now at a tipping point and a time for cultural choosing when it comes to physician-assisted killing (PAK). Note: This term, rather than "physician-assisted suicide," will be used primarily throughout this book because — as we will see many times — the killing of the person is explicitly or structurally coerced, or both. The full agency of physicians in contributing to the killing of an innocent person should therefore be emphasized, rather than the compromised agency of those who are perhaps pushed to suicide.

On the one hand, attempts to legalize the practice have failed even in deeply progressive American states and European countries. Again, given that we are at this tipping point for the culture, the following could change in a matter of weeks, but at the time of this writing, the following states and countries have formally rejected attempts to legalize PAK:

- Connecticut
- Maryland
- Virginia
- Massachusetts
- New Hampshire
- Illinois
- Minnesota
- The United Kingdom (big votes coming as of this writing)
- Ireland
- France
- Denmark
- Norway
- Sweden
- Finland

Some of these victories have been against a well-funded and stubborn opposition with significant culture power. Connecticut has fended off attempts to pass PAK for twelve straight years, and in 2024, the legislation was so thoroughly defeated that proponents didn't even bring it up in committee.[4] Also in 2024, deep-blue Maryland defeated it for the ninth year in a row.[5] And even as forces gathered to try to pass PAK in Illinois, the progressive editorial board of the *Chicago Tribune* came out against legalization.[6] The United Kingdom has faced attempts to pass PAK for many years now and continues to reject it.[7] Even the European Court of Human Rights made a 2024 ruling that PAK is not a human right.[8]

Many of these successful efforts against PAK have been buoyed by disability rights groups and clinical organizations. For instance, the American Association of People with Disabilities claims: "Assisted suicide is eugenics, and should never be praised or considered a viable alternative to providing disabled people with comprehensive, high-quality affordable medical care."[9] The American Medical Association, the standard-setting organization for contemporary medicine in the United States, despite repeated attempts to change its position to "for" or "neutral" with respect to PAK, is officially and very strongly against PAK, describing it as "fundamentally incompatible with the physician's role as healer."[10] At their June 2025 meeting, the AMA house of delegates overwhelmingly rejected making any changes to this position.

On the other hand, there has been considerable movement in the other direction. Spain and Italy have recently legalized PAK. Canada too, as we will see in the next chapter, has slid down the PAK slope incredibly fast in the last few years. American states such as New Jersey, California, Colorado, and New Mexico have also recently legalized PAK. As this book was being written, the Medical Society of New York changed its position from being against PAK to being in favor of it.[11] Very significant votes will likely take place soon in Arizona as well as in France.[12]

Again, we are at a turning point for the culture of the consumerist West when it comes to these matters, with strong and influential voices and powers clashing quite dramatically. In broad resistance to PAK, disability rights groups are joined by the Catholic Church and other religious institutions (including those belonging to Muslims, which have been very effective partners with Catholics in this regard[13]) that defend the inviolable dignity of the human person. Significantly, economically vulnerable populations, especially vulnerable populations of color, are broadly opposed to PAK (and distrustful of Western medicine's end-of-life practices generally[14]). Native and First Nations peoples are also often deeply opposed.[15]

Those broadly in support, by contrast, tend to be white and economically privileged. They tend to emphasize autonomy and power of the individual over interests such as the common good and concern for the most vulnerable. They tend to be highly educated — indeed, colleges and universities are primary places where arguments and strategies in support of PAK are incubated and promoted. (In a remarkable development, the University of Toronto recently appointed its first endowed chair in "End-of-Life Care and Medical Assistance in Dying."[16]) And last but certainly not least, those broadly in support often have eugenic or cost-related concerns, or both, related to their support of PAK.[17]

Does any of this sound historically familiar? Very similar shifts in thinking took place among elite, highly educated, and medical communities during the first four decades of the twentieth century, abating only after the horrors of the Holocaust.[18] Nazi Germany infamously launched an aggressive euthanasia program based on eugenics, often invoking the financial drain on the state posed by the *Lebensunwertes Leben*, or "lives unworthy of life." These included the mentally ill, the feeble-minded, and the demented elderly.[19] Though there was resistance in the German medical community at the time (in particular, Catholic nurses from the Sisters of Mercy of St. Vincent de Paul refused to participate in the program), nearly one in two physicians — a much higher percentage than in any other profession — joined the Nazi party. Physicians were also a whopping seven times more likely than other employed German males to join the SS.[20]

As the historian Ian Dowbiggin makes clear, much of the intellectual and ideological framework for what happened in the Holocaust was built by academics in the United States.[21] Eugenics — buoyed by moves toward secularization, utilitarianism, Darwinism, and support for some version of survival of the fittest — was simply the order of the day for many U.S. elites. Indeed, this era saw the formation of the American Eugenics Society and the Euthanasia Society of America.

Significantly, as in Germany, there was resistance to this movement in the United States, and much of it, again, came from the Catholic Church. Msgr. John Ryan, a U.S. scholar of Catholic social teaching, for instance, used the moral tradition of the Church to do battle with the American Eugenics Society.[22] Ryan was able to draw on the insights of the pope at the time as well, for just as support for eugenics and euthanasia were gaining momentum in the developed West, Pius XII released a countercultural encyclical calling eugenics a "grave crime" and "pernicious practice."[23]

Dowbiggin's history of euthanasia and PAK demonstrates that these battlelines are anything but accidental or novel. Both voluntary and unvoluntary euthanasia were unremarkable phenomena in pagan Greece and Rome — so much so that Dowbiggin suggests that the Hippocratic Oath, which forbids the practice, must have been understood as quite a countercultural document. Indeed, one of the many shifts that a dominant Christian culture produced was to a medical culture focused on the nonviolent example of Christ — a culture that, for instance, explicitly rejected the widespread pagan practice of euthanasia for disabled newborns. As Matthew 25 instructs us, Christians are to see Christ's Holy Face in the very marginalized populations most at risk of being discarded and killed this way. All things being equal, a culture adhering to gospel values will resist PAK, while a secularizing culture will be tempted to embrace it. We saw that in ancient Greece and Rome. We saw that in the United States and Germany during the first part of the twentieth century. And, despite a brief reprieve offered by righteous responses to the horrors of the Holocaust, continued secularization has brought to the contemporary West more eugenics, more utilitarianism, and more support for PAK.

Indeed, one of the most influential U.S. scholars and activists in support of PAK, Thaddeus Mason Pope, suggests that "what's next" for the practice in the United States will include massive expansion, including coverage of the practice by the federal government via Medicare.[24] The United States and other countries in the consumerist West now find themselves at a time for choosing. To answer the question posed by the title of this introduction: We are on the brink not only of making PAK broadly legal but of trapping the most vulnerable in structures and systems that will pressure them to end their lives prematurely and for reasons few of us want to think about. Indeed, especially as the horrors of the Holocaust fade from our cultural and institutional memories, we are finding ourselves dangerously close to where we were a century ago as a culture.

As we will see in more detail in the next chapter, perhaps the least understood fact about PAK is that requests for it are not so much from fear of pain and suffering. Rather, such requests are from fear that the sick, the disabled, and the dying will continue to feel ever more alone, useless, and unloved — basically the polar opposite of an approach that insists that they bear the Face of Christ in a special way, a way that demands our preferential attention. A central argument of this book is that a Catholic understanding of what it means to die well (and, by extension, what it means to live well — and for Catholic individuals and communities to help others to live and die well) provides an essential way of resisting the existential threat to human dignity posed by PAK.

Those of us who live in a eugenic culture of death and what Pope Francis named our "throwaway culture" do not know how to die well. Again, not least because it resists death's entering our social consciousness, our culture needs the help of the Catholic Church to recapture the idea of a good death. A Catholic understanding will, of course, build explicitly on both Scripture and Tradition, and this book will do so as well, diving into Jesus' paradigmatic example of how to die (and live) and the example of saints, monks, and Catholic health-care providers. The book challenges readers to live (and die) with these values and practices in mind: as individuals, as families, and as broader Church communities and institutions. One key is offered to us by the great St. Francis of Assisi himself: We are to praise God through our dying well and even to think of "Sister Death," a guest each of us will one day host for a very intimate visit.

It is always wrong to aim at the death of the innocent. This is what basic, foundational respect for fundamental human dignity and equality recognizes. These same commitments require resistance to structures and systems that make vulnerable people discardable when they are sick, disabled, or coming to the end of their lives. But at the same time, we need to recapture a culture that, far from denying the reality of death and dying, thinks about it regularly. Indeed, we must think about it so regularly that it fundamentally shapes how we live — and especially how we live together.

The Church (again, as individuals, as families, and as larger communities and institutions) must work to create a counterculture of thick, supportive relationships to help facilitate this. We must work to create a counterculture of encounter and hospitality to resist the eugenic culture of death and the consumerist throwaway culture. This is a central theme to which we'll be turning again and again in this book. In order to resist the evil of PAK, we need learn how to die well. In order to die well, we need to learn how to live well. In order to live well, we need to create positive and supportive relationships that explicitly resist the forces that lead to PAK.

And given the stakes of where we are in the consumerist West at this moment in history — given that we find ourselves on the brink of capitulation to PAK — the Church must have a profound sense of urgency in moving in these directions. This is an all-hands-on-deck moment that requires an all-of-the-above-approach — from our social justice ministries (sometimes identified with the Left or the progressive) to our pro-life ministries (sometimes identified with the Right or the conservative) and beyond.

The Church's moral and social vision, overall and in the main, is a single, unified whole that was made for a moment like the one we are facing. We cannot let secular Right-Left divisions in the Church keep us from meeting the moment. On this fundamental issue of justice for the most vulnerable, I urge those who might identify more with the social justice–centered Left to work with your Catholic brothers and sisters who identify differently. Your impulse and capacity to understand how human dignity is threatened by structures and systems will be essential if our resistance to PAK is going to be successful.

In resisting this fundamental attack on the inviolable goodness of human life, I urge those who identify more with the pro-life Right to work with your Catholic brothers and sisters who identify differently. A few years ago, Sister Constance of the Little Sisters of the Poor (a religious order dedicated to caring for the vulnerable elderly) wrote the author of this book the following email:

> In the face of increasingly dire prognostications about the shortage of elder care givers and the underfunding of services for seniors I am feeling compelled to write something informing our readers of this situation and what we need to do to reverse it as the population of elders rapidly grows. Something that always puzzles me is that "pro-life" as a term and a movement still seems to be hyper-focused on abortion and not end of life issues and care of the most vulnerable seniors. I wanted to ask someone knowledgeable in these issues

if my assessment is accurate, and if so, why. If it is not accurate, are you seeing people mobilizing on behalf of frail seniors, the disabled, etc.?

I have no doubt many readers have (or will have) a reaction to our current moment that will address Sister Constance's question. Your impulse and capacity to defend vulnerable human lives from deadly violence will be required if resistance to PAK is going to be successful.

But before bringing our combined resources as a Church together in this way, we need to better understand the culture that has produced PAK, and vice versa. All the good intentions in the world will be useless unless we understand the root cultural causes of what is going on here.

CHAPTER ONE

What Physician-Assisted Killing Reveals About Our Culture

The introduction to this book mentions the story of Brittany Maynard, a story whose influence cannot be overstated — both for its direct influence on the legalization of physician-assisted killing in California and for the larger discourse about PAK in the United States and other places influenced by U.S. discourse. Maynard received the tragic diagnosis of an inoperable and fatal brain tumor in 2014, when she was only twenty-nine years old, and her story is often the one that comes into our cultural consciousness when the issue of PAK comes up. "I wouldn't want to die in agony from a brain tumor either," many folks understandably conclude.

But any genuine debate over PAK must be informed by the facts, and the facts may not fit what has come into our cultural consciousness. The state of Oregon, which has had legal PAK since the 1990s, tracks the reasons why people request it. And get this: Physical pain and suffering don't even make the top five.[1] Here's a representative snapshot of the reasons reported:

1. Loss of autonomy (91.4 percent)
2. Decreased ability to engage in enjoyable activities (86.7 percent)
3. Loss of dignity (71.4 percent)
4. Loss of control of bodily functions (49.5 percent)
5. Becoming a burden on others (40 percent)

Don't believe the data from a single state? We find very similar results when we expand to other states,[2] and a study in Canada found something similar.[3] We will discuss more about issues related to race and social class later in this chapter (the study found, again, that PAK users are overwhelmingly white and economically privileged), but here let's note that the study found "loss of autonomy was the primary reason for their request. Other common reasons included the wish to avoid burdening others or losing dignity and the intolerability of not being able to enjoy one's life. Few patients cited inadequate control of pain or other symptoms." Studies in Europe have found something similar.[4]

Though we need to get better access to pain management for vulnerable populations (and data show that when PAK is introduced into a society, palliative care actually gets worse[5]), one of the main reasons physical pain doesn't make the top five is that, in the overwhelming majority of cases, palliative care (and especially palliative sedation) can control the pain. As we will see later in this book, hospice care in particular can control the pain in even the most difficult situations. No, there is something else going on here. Something else about our culture, something quite profound and disturbing, is revealed by the reasons people request PAK.

Pope Francis emphasized how our consumerist "throwaway culture" shapes so many of our assumptions and practices, particularly when it comes to what kinds of lives we consider worth living and what kinds of lives we think may (and perhaps should) be thrown away. Perhaps no practice better reveals the throwaway culture than assisted suicide. It is a practice aimed not primarily at those facing and fearing terrible physical pain but, rather, at those facing and fearing loss of their autonomy, loss of enjoyable activities, loss of their dignity, and (revealingly) being a burden on others.

If you're thinking that this list of reasons sounds suspiciously as if they apply in a particular way to those who are not able-bodied, you're on the right track here. In fact, this list reveals quite clearly why so many disabled communities are fierce critics of the so-called right to die. Far too often, the impulse behind the right to die implies that the lives of the disabled are not worth living. Again, when thinking about these matters, many disabled people have, very much in the center of their minds, questions like the one raised in the introduction: "Why do we keep severely mentally disabled people alive, other than the fact that they're human?"

Our throwaway culture assumes that, because these lives are not useful to our consumer-driven economic system (indeed, they are net burdens on it), they are the kinds of lives that can and probably should be discarded via PAK. This book absolutely insists that we must build and live in a counterculture that affirms the goodness of those who have lost their autonomy, who have had enjoyable activities taken from them, who feel as if their lives no longer have dignity — perhaps because they feel as if they are a burden on others.

The introduction to this book mentioned that the Church — as individuals, as families, and as larger communities and institutions — must play a central role in working to create a counterculture of thick, supportive relationships. Communities constituted by encounter, hospitality, and accompaniment — all themes of the Pope Francis pontificate — will be essential to help people in these contexts (contexts that all of those reading these pages are likely to face!) to learn to live and die in a way that resists the evil of PAK. Again, that is the central argument of this book: To resist the existential threat to human dignity posed by PAK, we must rediscover the Catholic understanding of what it means to die well and, by extension, what it means to live well and what it means for Catholic individuals and communities to help others to live and die well.

We will dive more deeply into what this means toward the end of this chapter and throughout the rest of the book. But first, let's focus on the reality of how PAK serves our Western consumerist throwaway culture. Canada gives us a very poignant example.

What's Going On in Canada?

Lots of attention has been paid to Canada since the country legalized physician-assisted killing in 2016.[6] At first, it was available only for adults suffering badly and incurably at the end of their lives. Just four years later, however, the logic of the arguments made in favor of PAK began to take over. If one really is in total control over one's body and one's life and one's death — so the argument goes — then who really has the right to limit those choices?

PAK became legal in Canada in 2020 even for people whose death was not reasonably foreseeable, thus (among other things) extending the practice to the nondying disabled. Those with physical disabilities are routinely killed via PAK in Canada. To give just one of many examples, a nondying patient with spina bifida was asked twice, and unprompted, if she wanted PAK.[7]

But the government has decided to pause killing people purely because of mental illness until 2027.[8] Significantly, this pause is the result of the activists' warnings about the social disaster for people with mental illness if Canadian culture decides that being mentally ill is an understandable and even a good and expected reason to seek PAK. Unfortunately for other vulnerable populations in Canada, the social disaster is already upon them.

Consider the story of sixty-six-year-old truck driver Normand Meunier.[9] In 2022, he suffered a severe spinal-cord injury that paralyzed his arms and legs, thus requiring a particular kind of mattress to avoid pressure sores when he lies down for extended periods of time. In the winter of 2024, Normand was admitted into intensive care with a third respiratory virus in as many months but was put on a stretcher for four days. His partner advocated for a change, but none was forthcoming, and because the medical staff failed to rotate his body properly, Normand developed a terrible pressure sore on his buttocks, one that exposed the bone and was incredibly painful. The prognosis for healing was not great, and plus, said Normand, "I don't want to be a burden." He was killed via PAK on March 29, 2024.

Or how about Alan Nichols, a man with a history of depression and other medical issues that did not threaten his life?[10] He was hospitalized in June 2019 in part because of fears that he might be suicidal — an interesting fact because, as was mentioned in the introduction to this book, a significant part of Western culture still presumes that it is bad for people to kill themselves. But while Alan was under the care of his medical team, he submitted a request for PAK and was, in fact, killed. The only medical condition listed as a reason for his request? Hearing loss. His family made a police report, insisting that he didn't have the capacity to make this decision, that he wasn't taking his medications and wasn't using the implants that allowed him to hear. His brother Gary described what happened rather directly:

"Alan was basically put to death."[11]

A fifty-one-year-old woman known as "Sophia" said, "The government sees me as expendable trash, a complainer, useless and a pain in the a**."[12] Her complaint? The public housing in which she lived contained chemicals to which she had severe sensitivities. Her friends, supporters, and even doctors tried to get her alternative housing. She wrote desperate letters to government officials begging for help and explaining that she couldn't live in her current environment. When no help was forthcoming, she requested and received PAK. Sophia hoped that her death might spur change — but, diabolically, the public attention her case received has caused more people with multiple chemical sensitivities (MCS) to inquire about PAK.

These are terrible stories in which vulnerable people get the message that, though they are not dying, they would be better off dead. Many more examples from the Canadian experience could be mentioned here.[13] Veterans seeking assistance through Veterans Affairs Canada (one who asked for post-traumatic stress disorder treatment and another who asked that a wheelchair ramp be built into her home) were asked if PAK would be a better option for them, though neither was dying.[14] Then there was the sixty-three-year-old man who had been waiting in terrible pain for spinal fusion surgery for a whopping eighteen years. Saying, "I am fed opioids and left to kill myself," he requested and was approved for PAK.[15] A forty-four-year-old woman who was denied home health care for her degenerative disease decided to be forthright about what actually killed her: "Ultimately it was not a genetic disease that took me out, it was a system. There is a desperate need for change. That is the sickness that causes so much suffering. Vulnerable people need help to survive. I could have had more time if I had more help."[16]

The largest and most progressive newspaper in Canada understandably described what we have just encountered in these stories as "'Hunger Games' style social Darwinism."[17] And the trends there appear to be accelerating. Despite the stories above serving as clear warning signs, from 2022 to 2023, the number of PAK deaths in Canada did not decline but instead rose by more than 30 percent.[18] As of 2022, more than 4 percent of all deaths in Canada are due to PAK, trailing only accidents, cancer, heart disease, and COVID-19.

Has Canada reached the bottom of the slippery slope yet? The continuing debate over PAK for the mentally ill suggests that the answer is no. Indeed, everyone from disability lawyers to psychiatrists and bioethicists are arguing for including these populations in the name of inclusivity[19] and equality, giving them "the same options as all other Canadians."[20] The views of young people in Canada are also a reason to think the country has not reached the bottom of the slope: When asked whether one agrees that "disability" or "poverty" are reasons to allow PAK, eighteen- to thirty-four-year-olds were the age group most likely to answer in the affirmative. Sixty percent of young people agree with PAK because of disability, and 41 percent consider poverty to be a legitimate reason for PAK.[21]

Europe

The Netherlands, via a law passed in 2001, was the first country in Europe to decriminalize physician-assisted killing. By 2016 the Netherlands had reached Canadian numbers, with 4 percent of all Dutch deaths coming by way of PAK. They initially tried to curtail the effect of the law by limiting it to those over twelve years old (so that they could reasonably consent to the procedure) and to those whose suffering is unbearable, with zero chance for improvement. These limitations would not be in place for long. In 2003, the Netherlands made PAK available for all children, doing away with any reasonable sense of consent on their behalf.[22] And take a look at this list of reasons people in the

Netherlands have been killed:

- Suffering as a result of sexual assault[23]
- Suffering as a result of body image disorder (anorexia nervosa)[24]
- Suffering as a result of depression[25]
- Suffering as a result of autism[26]
- Suffering (either fear of future suffering or current suffering) as a result of dementia[27]

More will be said below about the particular instance of PAK for dementia, but for now, let's turn to the country of Belgium, which legalized PAK in 2002 but opened it up to nonconsenting minors nearly ten years before the Netherlands. They have been on a similar slippery slope — and not just away from terminal illness and unbearable, unchangeable suffering due to mental illnesses (such as depression and body image disorder) but in the numbers themselves. In 2002, only 24 Belgians were killed via PAK. In 2024, that number was 3,991.[28]

Perhaps even more disturbing, however, is the move in Belgium to consider "polypathology" as a legitimate reason for requesting PAK. A study appearing in the *Journal of Medicine and Philosophy* (*JMP*) defined the term this way: "the co-occurrence of multiple chronic or acute diseases and medical conditions within one person."[29] These include "reduced eyesight which could result in increased social isolation, polyarthritis, reduced hearing to complete deafness that inhibits the person's ability for human contact, early stage dementia, and incontinence."

If this sounds an awful lot like "getting old" to you, that's because it is. PAK in Belgium is legal just for people who go through the aging process. The *JMP* article noted that 17.4 percent of all cases in Belgium were related to "polypathology," but some experts suggest that underreporting means the real number is much larger.³⁰

Both the Netherlands and Belgium have seen recent efforts to expand PAK to those who are simply "tired of life," efforts that, at least from the outside, appear to have failed. But the *JMP* authors suggest that PAK for "polypathology" may be little different in practice from what these proposed laws are after. Indeed, it is not difficult to imagine someone who is losing his or her hearing and eyesight requesting and receiving PAK on the basis of "polypathology" — especially when one considers that otherwise healthy, deaf adult Belgian twins were killed by PAK because they feared becoming blind.³¹

As mentioned in the introduction, the United Kingdom is one of several places in Europe that has, at the time of writing this book,³² refused to cave to a culture of PAK — not least due to the influence of disability rights organizations. So when a thirty-one-year-old British horse-riding star had a terrible accident that confined her to a wheelchair, well, one might think that the culture would be forced to make space for her, give her alternative ways to flourish, and uphold the value of those with disabilities. The only problem is that countries such as Switzerland offer PAK "tourism," where people like Caroline March can travel to die by PAK.³³ And in March 2024, she traveled outside the UK for precisely this reason. In a letter, Caroline shared that:

- Ideally, she didn't want to give a defense of her decision, but she wanted to try to silence her critics.
- She was not depressed at the time, but she had been depressed in the past and also had "crippling body dysmorphia and anxiety."
- COVID isolation was her "savior" and got her to work on herself.
- After her spinal cord injury, she never sunk into that hole.

- She was very angry that all of her hard work wasn't going anywhere.
- She described herself as "feral, a complete rogue, someone that thrives on spontaneity" — and now she could not be that self in the way it used to work.
- She hated asking for help and it "destroy[ed]" her to watch others "do my jobs."
- She needed risk: "that dopamine hit and the threat of danger" — "adrenaline hits are my addiction."
- She always said that if she couldn't have the quality of life she wanted, then this was the route she would take.
- She admitted that some would call her selfish and that she probably was being a spoiled brat, but she had "always been one of those, so why change now?"

We don't know where Caroline died, but it is likely that she went to Dignitas, a Swiss organization that provides the opportunity for people like her to leave countries that protect vulnerable lives from the pressures of legal PAK.

In that same month, Dignitas killed Hal Malchow by PAK as well.[34] Hal, a longtime campaign consultant for the Democratic Party in the United States, was seventy-two years old and had been showing the early symptoms of dementia resulting from Alzheimer's disease. He had been a member of a very privileged class for most of his life, and one of his friends said it didn't surprise him that he wanted to die as he had lived: on his own terms.

A Culture of Loneliness and Isolation

In some ways, we should not be surprised that loneliness and isolation are revealed to be hallmarks of a culture that finds itself at risk for PAK. This is what so much of the consumerist West sells: appeals to individual autonomy and freedom, especially when it comes to the social entanglements that being "dependent on others" require of us. This kind of independence has always been a harmful illusion, and it betrays the inherently finite, dependent, and social nature of human beings; but it is particularly pernicious today, when applications on our glowing rectangles connect us virtually with "friends" and fool us into thinking these cost-free, fleeting relationships are all we need to be flourishing human beings. Indeed, Westerners (especially men) have fewer and fewer actual thick, supportive friendships and spend less time with the real friends they do have.[35]

Remember how the Netherlands is killing people with autism and other intellectual disabilities via PAK? A British study found that in 77 percent of these cases, the people noted that loneliness played a central role in how they cited their unbearable pain. Many Western cultures — not least due to our cultural myths about individual autonomy and independence — tend to create social conditions in which living alone becomes the most acceptable thing to do, even (and perhaps especially) when one is sick, elderly, or in the process of dying.

This problem is particularly acute for people in the United States. At about the age of seventy-six, for instance, it becomes more likely that an American will be living alone rather than with a spouse.[36] We will focus explicitly on the caregiving context below, but one thing that the COVID-19 pandemic revealed was just how badly we treat those who are elderly, sick, or in the process of dying. Human beings are created to be their most flourishing selves when in deep, profound social networks, but the pandemic forced us out of our comfort zones of denial and made us look at the horrific and indeed torturous existence these populations face as radically isolated and lonely individuals.[37]

People who live isolated lives have significantly more problems (health and otherwise) than those who are socially connected.[38] They die younger, for starters. Indeed, people who are socially isolated have problems and outcomes comparable to severe obesity or smoking fifteen cigarettes per day. Being unmarried or having no close friends makes one far more likely to die of cancer. In addition, social isolation activates parts of the brain associated with physical pain and predicts fatigue and depression.

Our Contemporary Medical Context

It would be surprising if these kinds of trends in the broader culture didn't translate into medical contexts as well — especially since physicians tend to be more privileged members of our communities and therefore more likely to reflect a privileged point of view that emphasizes individual autonomy, control, independence, freedom, and so forth. But, in addition to this, physicians tend to have values about the quality of life that are quite different from those of the disabled and other more vulnerable populations.[39]

By the numbers, for instance, physicians rate the quality of life of their disabled patients worse than the patients do themselves.[40] Something similar has been found in their attitudes toward disabled or sick adolescents and their families.[41] Every so often, we see articles insisting that these vulnerable populations learn how to die "like doctors"[42] — that is, without fighting for a life that is diminished with regard to autonomy, control, independence, and freedom; without fighting for a life that is diminished in its "quality." But average patients, though this surprises many privileged physicians, prefer length of life to quality of life.

Unfortunately, however, when patients think about extending the length of their lives, it takes place in a social and medical culture that presumes social isolation. This culture presumes that patients will be cut out of the very relationships (even relationships of dependence) for which human beings are made. It is a technocratic, conveyor-belt-like experience that does not honor the dignity of the human person as embedded in relationship. Lydia S. Dugdale, Silberberg Professor of Medicine at Columbia University, based the following description on her experience in taking care of terminal patients: "Who wouldn't shudder at the thought of languishing in a sterile medical ward, too sick to escape, imprisoned by illness, dependent on futuristic machines, at the mercy of an anonymous throng of health care professionals?" After noting that about eight in ten Americans prefer to die at home, she gives a moving account of why that is:

> There remains a certain constancy to home life — pets and people, to be sure, but also *that* chair, *that* painting, *that* perennial plant. The home is where we feast and celebrate, weep and mourn, sit and stare. ... Home accepts us at our most authentic. Home embraces us, silently consoling us with the knowledge that we belong to *this* home. Why would we die anywhere else?[43]

Well, the answer is that, for most of the history of our culture, no one really thought of dying anywhere else. Hospitals were invented by Catholic institutions mainly to care for people who had no homes or no family to care for them: the very poor, travelers, the elderly living alone.

With the Industrial Revolution and the advent of Western-style capitalism in the nineteenth century, however, this culture was disrupted. Families would come to feel significant pressure to change the balance between work and family life to fit this new cultural context, especially by moving to cities, the new centers of wealth and jobs. During this time, notes Dugdale, hospitals shifted from places of dreaded horrors to "a workplace for the production of health." Medicine, instead of conforming itself to the domestic life, began to professionalize, compete in financial markets, and offer products that customers would come to them to purchase. Hospitals lost their stigma, proliferated, and became moneymakers.

Indeed, through expensive, profit-generating technology, these new health-care institutions both (1) offered their customers the illusion that they could save them from death and (2) dramatically reduced the care responsibilities on families and communities overburdened and even destroyed by industrialized capitalism. Caring for loved ones in one's home is difficult enough when one is genuinely free to do it, but when one needs to work sixty hours a week in the local factory to pay the rent, it becomes something close to impossible. Hospitals "freed up" family members to work as the market in this new context required them to, but very often at the cost of caregiving for family members and other close members of the local community.

Over time, this new social model led to practices related to dying and death that — while serving the interests of powerful moneymakers quite well — served patients and our broader culture quite poorly. As mentioned in the introduction, our culture's capacity to deny the reality of dying and death came in large part from its capacity to force these profound realities out of our homes and communities, where they came into contact with the practices and rhythms of day-to-day life. These new and isolating practices offered a false (though revenue-generating) fantasy of being rescued from death while depriving folks of the gift of dying at home; of dying in ways that were deeply connected to how they lived — connected to loved ones, loved things, loved communities, and loved local institutions.

Our Contemporary Caregiving Context

It is interesting to note that many of the terrible cases of physician-assisted killing in Canada involved structures that pushed people out of their homes and into unfamiliar, understaffed assisted-living facilities. Just as patients prefer to die at home, patients also prefer to live out their final years and months at home.⁴⁴ But the structures of our system, as mentioned above, also push people out of their homes and into assisted-living facilities.

Just as our consumerist throwaway culture refuses to face the realities of death and dying, it similarly refuses to really face the realities of growing old and more dependent. And it refuses to face these realities in a very similar way: by putting those who are growing old and more dependent into care facilities disconnected from our homes and daily lives. Once again, this "frees up" family members to go to work and be good Western-style consumers. And now, diabolically, these cultural expectations have been established over multiple centuries, such that older adults have been conditioned to look at the older model — the one in which aging, caregiving, dying, and death are centered in the home and the local community — as being a burden on others: one of the central reasons given for requesting PAK.

Another key reason given for choosing PAK is fear of the loss of enjoyable activities, such as regular social contact and gatherings with families and friends. Except for the most well-funded institutions, caregiving institutions in most Western contexts isolate older adults in a way that turns their lives into desperate attempts to pass the time. Some have gotten to the point of turning to AI-powered robots to fool these vulnerable populations into believing that someone is around to interact with them and that they matter enough for someone to have regular conversation with them.⁴⁵

Disabled populations in these contexts also very often receive care that is totally inadequate. Indeed, probes are currently underway in the UK to try to explain why life-saving treatment has been withheld from disabled people in certain care homes.⁴⁶ There is a special danger here for people living with dementia. Our care institutions in the West are already overburdened — indeed, a *New York Times* investigation found that high percentages of residents in nursing homes are given dangerous "chemical straitjackets" to keep them docile.[47] But, if current trends continue, the number of people with dementia is going to double in twenty years and triple in thirty years.

It is truly frightening to think about what will happen to these populations in a consumerist throwaway culture if we do not change course. Here's one disturbing example from the Netherlands (and we can expect more like it): A patient requested PAK when she was first diagnosed with dementia, but she was not set to be killed until the disease progressed. Sickeningly, she woke up after taking the deadly drug in her coffee and, apparently resisting the procedure, had to be physically restrained by the doctor and her family in order for the killing to be completed. The doctor was cleared of any wrongdoing.[48]

It is interesting to note that many immigrants from non-Western contexts find what we do to our elderly, disabled, or dying relatives in the secularized, consumerist West to be unthinkable. They were raised in cultures far more connected with religious traditions, with structures and systems so different from our own that they consider our practices with regard to aging, dying, and death deeply, profoundly unjust.

Indeed, and to bring us back to the central topic of the book, Pope Francis offered a difficult but necessary critique of our culture: "How many times are the elderly discarded with an attitude of abandonment, which is actually real and hidden euthanasia! It is the result of a throw-away culture which is so harmful to our world. We are all called to oppose this poisonous, throw away culture!"[49]

The Upshot of This Culture

How would you feel if, next year, as will happen for millions and millions in the consumerist West, you were given an early-onset-dementia diagnosis? What if — formed and taught by the culture outlined in this chapter — you saw a future in which you would be removed from your home, isolated in an institution, engaged primarily by robot "caregivers" and "friends," given substandard treatment and care, and be dependent on strangers to bear your burdens? What if you knew that you would very rarely see your family or friends, go to church, or otherwise interact with your community? What if it was likely that you would eventually be given a dangerous "chemical straitjacket" and forget the names of your loved ones? What if this would also cost you, your spouse, your family, and perhaps our social safety nets a ton of money?

Might you be tempted to seek physician-assisted killing to avoid this future? We've seen that this process is well underway in Canada, the Netherlands, Belgium, and Switzerland. Soon after California legalized PAK, the *Los Angeles Times* ran an opinion piece calling for it to be accessed by people with dementia who are not dying.[50] And 2024 saw a formal attempt to pass in that state updated legislation that explicitly permit PAK in this context.[51]

Yes, we are a culture on the brink, but it seems clear that we are about to go over the edge if we simply accept the status quo. If things stay as they are, California, other U.S. states, and many other Western countries will "free up" their citizens and residents to "choose" to end their lives via PAK. Those who enact these policies will do so in the name of autonomy and choice, even though many who will use it will either explicitly or implicitly be coerced into such actions by structures and systems of a throwaway culture we largely choose to ignore.

Happily, taking a clear look at this culture (something that, again, is so rarely done as we deny these uncomfortable realities) suggests many kinds of responses that can resist our culture's slide toward PAK — responses that can pull us back from the brink by offering solutions to these admittedly difficult problems.

Christ, His Church, and Building a Counterculture

It is no accident, again, that our slouch toward physician-assisted killing — and the throwaway culture that has led to it — has coincided with the erosion of Christian assumptions and institutions in our secularized culture. We need to engage the embarrassment of cultural riches from our ancient traditions in order to relearn how to live and die well. We must see dying as intimately connected to how we live, refusing the radical break the current culture makes between the two. Significantly, this means leading a life in which death is meditated upon in the great Christian tradition of *memento mori* — not just once a year, on Ash Wednesday, but as a central part of one's everyday life.

As Michael Connelly notes in his book *The Journey's End*, we should see aging and dying within the entire scope of our lives and meditate on it such that *it helps us understand what our lives are ultimately about*.[52] And this very clearly includes the fact that we are pilgrims, fully present in (but not of) this world — with a destination that goes well beyond it. With this notion firmly in hand, we can begin to resist the idea that aging, dying, and death are merely enemies to be dreaded and resisted at any cost (again, in ways and through structures that benefit and enrich some of our culture's most powerful constituencies) and to embrace the fact that they are, in some sense, gifts from God, without which it is nearly impossible to make sense of what is ultimately true.

Aging, dying, and death become absurd matters to contemplate if we accept the mythos of our secularizing consumer culture that we are in autonomous control of our lives and that we invent our own stories about what our lives are ultimately about and what is true "for us." The realities of aging, dying, and death (the futile, grasping attempts of the techno-immortalists notwithstanding[53]) reveal that such culture myths are ultimately and obviously nonsense. Indeed, this is clearly one of the primary reasons why those who are the most privileged in our culture are at such pains to do all they can to deny these realities: We want to pretend for as long as we can that we are in control. Recall that this place of control is where so many are coming from when pursuing PAK. Though some vulnerable populations (who know they are not in control) end up caught up in the structures that legalized PAK creates, typical supporters and users come from quite privileged backgrounds — backgrounds that can often fool them into thinking they are in control of their lives. Dugdale notes that they tend to be "white, married or widowed, college educated, and insured" folks who attempt to maintain their sense of control and security in the face of an unpredictable dying process. PAK, she says, "provides an escape route for those who do not wish to fight death — but still want control."[54]

Another way in which PAK serves the control fantasies of privileged populations comes from the perspective of those who don't want to face the difficulties and (from a certain point of view) absurdities of the death and dying of their loved ones. In such cases, PAK is less about acquiescing to the desire for control of the aging, sick, or dying person and more about serving the desire for control of the healthy. And indeed, in some circumstances, the two are intertwined. Consider, for instance, the following pro-PAK advertisement via a poster on the London subway: an attractive woman is leaping into the air with the following in big block letters, "My dying wish is that my family won't have to see me suffer, and I won't have to."[55]

Monotheists have a word for seeking control in this way and putting oneself (or anything else) in the place of God: *idolatry*. But we have seen another kind of idolatry on display in this chapter: the seeking of control in ways that use technology to extend one's life and fight death at any cost. This is especially problematic when, again, doing so disconnects the aging and dying process from one's life broadly understood. Those of us who follow Christ must never aim at the death of the innocent (including ourselves), but we must acknowledge that putting life extension ahead of other goods can also be idolatrous. The witness of the great martyrs of old, and of the Son of God on the cross, sit in clear judgment against attempts to live as long as we possibly can for any reason.

A Christian vision will find a via media between these two idolatrous extremes. Death is never to be sought as good and can rightly be resisted. (As we will focus on in some detail in the next chapter, Our Lord did pray in the Garden of Gethsemane that the cup pass from him; and earlier in the Gospel, he reacted with startling grief and anger when his best friend died.) But when death does come for us, we are to understand and accept her as a guest and even a gift from God. The great Saint Francis even offers a prayer of praise to God for "Sister Bodily Death."

The only way such a prayer makes sense is if death is understood as a way of illuminating the meaning of the story of our broader life, including eternal life. And the only way that this understanding of death makes sense is if we understand — and are formed by the understanding — that what it means to die well is an extension of what it means to live well.

And what does it mean to live well in this context? That is what the rest of this book is about. We will first focus on Christ — the way, the truth, and the life in all things — including what it means to incorporate one's death into one's life, and vice versa. We will also learn from key Catholic saints and especially Catholic friars and monks (of yesterday and today) who have kept a Gospel-centered countercultural vision alive even in the midst of our throwaway culture. And we will take a look at Catholic care homes and hospices that are doing their best to live out this countercultural vision as well. The final third of the book will explore and suggest ways in which individuals, families, and Church communities and institutions can learn from both our tradition and our current best practices to pull back from the brink of PAK.

It will look different in different contexts, but we can already point to several unifying themes and ideas that will be present in virtually every single one:

- Human life is good for its own sake; the fundamental dignity and equal value of every human life comes from being made in the image and likeness of God, not because of some capacity for this or that trait.
- Human beings are inherently finite, dependent, and social creatures; this means we must reject the harmful illusion that we are autonomous individuals who can somehow overcome our finitude.
- We must consistently keep our death front of mind, such that it fundamentally shapes how we live — both in this life and with an eye to the next.
- We must give up on the harmful illusions of autonomy and control that lead to the idolatrous extremes of (1) fighting for extended life at any cost and (2) responding to dying by taking death into one's own hands (or pushing another in that direction) — both of which misunderstand the dignity of the human person.
- It is important that we resist death when appropriate but also discern the time to accept and even welcome death as a gift from God (again, as part of a choice about how to live — rather than as a choice to die).
- In both living and dying, we must recognize the central importance of a supportive, real, embodied community, on multiple levels of need (material, so-

cial, spiritual).
- We must focus on a counterculture of encounter and hospitality as the antidote to our consumerist throwaway culture, which hides and (often violently) discards those whose dignity is inconvenient for the powerful.
- We need to have a willingness to show true compassion — to suffer with the suffering. For their part, those who are suffering must not see this as heaping burdens on others but, rather, as the give-and-take that comes with living in a true community, in which we give others opportunities to love.
- We must always look through a lens that gives special priority to the most vulnerable, the least among us, who bear the Holy Face of Christ in a special way: the poor, the disabled, the widow and the orphan, the racial minority — and, of course, the aging, the sick, and the dying.

But Christians come to know what is ultimately true not via abstract principles but through engagement with the person and love of Christ himself. And that is what we will turn to in the next chapter.

CHAPTER TWO

The Example of Christ

There is a centuries-old and stubbornly consistent critique of Catholic approaches to almost any issue. And it goes something like this: "Where's Jesus?" For a Church that proclaims a reading from the Gospels at every Mass and claims that the Real Presence of Christ in the Eucharist is the "source and summit of the Christian life," this may seem like an odd critique, but sometimes it hits home. Though Jesus built and instituted the Church to continue to proclaim the Gospel and make disciples of all nations — and sent the Holy Spirit to continue to inspire the Church to grow in wisdom and holiness in light of the signs of the times — some ideas and initiatives with a Catholic veneer are really up to something quite different. One indication that this may be the case is that the life and teachings of Jesus are either nowhere to be found, or they are invoked with such a thin level of detail ("He was about peace and love, man!") that they have no specific relation to the particular person of Jesus and the things he said and did.

Happily, an authentically Catholic approach to death and dying has much to engage in the life and teaching of Jesus. Indeed, the Church — as we will see in the coming chapters — has a long history of thinking about death and dying and has consistently put Jesus at the center of this reflection. This chapter will first engage Jesus' focus on human dignity in ways that are central to our goals in this book. It will then pivot explicitly to how often Jesus focused on how death (for both himself and his followers) should shape our lives. The chapter will then draw a tight focus on the final days of Jesus' life as offering us quite specific, and sometimes difficult, insights into the questions being raised by this book. Finally, we will explore the views of death, dying, and physician-assisted killing held by those who bear the Holy Face of Christ in special ways as the least among us.

Jesus on Human Dignity

Allen Verhey, the great theologian and bioethicist, wrote an important book that played a key role in shaping this chapter: *The Christian Art of Dying: Learning from Jesus*.[1] He rightly insists that we must not disconnect very specific and important details of Jesus' dying and death from the life that had gone before it. Verhey puts it so beautifully that it is worth quoting:

> We must not forget that Jesus came announcing that the good future of God was at hand, that God was about to act to end the rule of sin and death. We must not forget that Jesus made that good future present and real in his works of healing and in his words of blessing. When he healed the sick, when his restored the possessed to self-control, when he raised the dead, the good future of God made its power felt.

We know from the book of Genesis and other sources from Scripture and Tradition that human life is dignified — that is, good for its own sake — because it is made in the image and likeness of God (and not because of some capacity for this or that trait). Jesus kicks it up a notch in his foundational parable of the sheep and the goats in Matthew 25, where he highlights the most marginalized, those without the capacities or traits that give one value and standing. Not only do these human beings bear the image of God, just as any other human being does, but we are told that they should be given special consideration. And in Jesus' day-to-day choices, we find this truth lived with excellence.

Who were the most marginalized and despised people of the Roman-occupied land of Jesus' day? One could make a strong case for the Jewish tax collectors, who collaborated with the imperial forces in depriving the local people of their livelihood — and also (often) skimming quite a bit off the top for themselves. Jesus' response was to call just such a person, Matthew, from sitting in his tax booth to join his special inner circle of twelve.

Jesus also made a point of counterculturally and regularly engaging women, including women who had major cultural strikes against them — public sexual sinners, such as the woman at the well, the woman who anointed his feet with expensive oil, and the woman caught in the act of adultery. Jesus also engaged with despised foreign women, such as the Canaanite who asked for mercy and healing for her demon-possessed daughter. Moved by the woman's faithful persistence, Jesus healed her daughter. He also focused on ministering to another marginalized and often despised group: the sick and the disabled. He cleansed lepers, gave sight to the blind, commanded the paralyzed to walk, restored withered hands, opened the ears and mouths of people unable to hear and speak, and much more. Again, focused on those despised by his culture, Jesus even healed the servant of a Roman centurion — a member of the very force behind the land's occupation.

Predictably, this caused those who had power in the culture to grumble and plot against him, explicitly arguing that because Jesus ate with tax collectors, prostitutes, and sinners, he could not be a holy man sent by God. But Jesus reveals a Gospel that turns such cultural expectations on their head. Indeed, he insists that it is those who are most privileged in the culture who have the most to worry about when it comes to their holiness, for they often have attitudes, temptations, and expectations that put their salvation in jeopardy. Holiness comes, instead, through making oneself small instead of big, weak instead of strong, and through becoming the servant of those the culture discards as insignificant or even dangerous.

Jesus' life calls us, his followers, to live out what Pope Francis called a culture of encounter and hospitality directed at these populations — one that serves as a Gospel-shaped antidote to a throwaway culture that would prefer that these populations simply didn't exist.

Death Front of Mind

One of the key principles for having a good death — one that can resist physician-assisted killing — is that we must consistently keep our own death front of mind, such that it fundamentally shapes how we live. And this is certainly something that has deep and profound roots in the example of Jesus. Indeed, especially in the Gospels of Mark and Matthew, the first message Jesus preaches is about ultimate matters: "The kingdom of God is at hand! Repent and believe in the Gospel!" (Mk 1:15; see Mt 3:2).

The earliest Christian communities, recalling these words of Jesus, would likely have understood them to refer to the Second Coming of Christ, an event they expected in their lifetimes. But as the years and decades went by, and community members started dying, a new approach and interpretation developed. Indeed, in his First Letter to the Thessalonians, Paul is apparently trying to address precisely these concerns and assures his readers that the dead will rise with Christ as well. Indeed, the Catholic Church connects this opening message of Jesus with an awareness of our death by invoking them on Ash Wednesday. Sometimes, when the priest places the ashes on our foreheads in the Sign of the Cross, we hear the words "Remember you are dust and to dust you shall return." But at other times we are told, "Repent and believe in the Gospel."

Throughout the Gospels, we see that Jesus is keen to warn us that we know neither the day nor the hour when death is coming for us, and therefore we need to be hyperaware that this moment could come at any time — and to live as though that is the case. Indeed, he specifically warns us about this through the parable of the rich fool, who builds huge barns for himself to store up all his goods, with the goal of resting, eating, drinking, and making merry. The hammer comes down later in the parable when God says to him, "You fool! You will die this very night!" (see Lk 12:16–20).

The fact of our pending death focuses our minds and hearts on what Jesus insists should be the central values in our lives. Explaining the parable of the rich fool, Jesus insists that we are not to worry about storing up accumulated goods but, rather, are to give to the poor and to make sure our hearts are focused on the treasure of heaven, of the kingdom of God. In that sense, as we saw in the previous chapter, we can understand death as a good thing. But as we also saw in that chapter, a Catholic understanding of death is complex and messy — because death, in another sense, is absolutely not a good thing. We know this from the book of Genesis: Death comes from sin and thus is not part of the original Peaceable Kingdom of Eden, nor will it be part of the recapitulation of that kingdom at the end of time, which will see no more suffering or death.

But we can also see this from Jesus himself, who, many times throughout the Gospels, reacts to death as a great evil to be avoided. We have already discussed Jesus' healing acts of ministry, several of which saved the lives of people who were ill. But no fewer than three times in the Gospels, we see Jesus explicitly raise to life someone who has died. In Luke 7 he raises the only son of a widow after being moved with pity for her situation. In all three synoptic Gospels, we learn that Jesus raised from the dead the daughter of a leader of the local synagogue. In the Gospel of Mark, Jesus' command to the girl to "get up!" is recorded in the original Aramaic, suggesting the story comes directly from the original oral tradition. In both Mark and Luke, we experience Jesus' earthly and moving concern for the girl, who, now alive, should be given something to eat (see Mk 5:21–24, 35–43; Lk 8:40–42, 49–55).

But by far, the best-known story of Jesus' responding to death as an evil comes with the death of his close friend Lazarus, a death that obviously touched him very deeply. Indeed, as the Gospel of John recounts his reaction, it offers the shortest verse in the New Testament (and, in some translations, the whole Bible): "Jesus wept" (11:35). John also reveals another emotion that Jesus has, this time upon encountering the others who were weeping for Lazarus. We are told via the *Catholic Study Bible* (NAB) translation that Jesus "became perturbed and deeply troubled" (11:33). Indeed, the note in the *Study Bible* suggests that the literal translation is that Jesus "snorted in spirit," which is a "striking phrase in Greek."[2]

In Jesus, then, we find the great tension in how to understand death. In some very significant ways, death is a good thing, for it can illuminate the meaning and story of our broader life, including eternal life. But at the same time, death can and should, in the right context, be resisted and mourned. Indeed, we see this quite directly in the story of how Jesus approached his own death.

Jesus' Death

Though it is disputed by Scripture scholars, what we read in the Lord's Prayer as "lead us not into temptation" is often translated as "do not subject us to the final test" (Mt 6:13). This invokes the Church's memory of the final test to which Jesus was subjected as he followed the way of the cross leading to his death. Now, Verhey is keen and right to warn us that Jesus' calling and death are different from ours. His death was the vehicle of salvation, and ours is not. He is the Son of God, and we are not. Nevertheless, there are many things for us to learn from Jesus' death.

First, he went to Jerusalem knowing that death would likely be the result of his trip. Indeed, he had been telling his disciples at various points in his life that the Son of Man had to suffer and die. Few of us are similarly called, but there's a truth to which Jesus is witnessing here: Life is a great good, but life is not the greatest good. We must not extend it at any cost but, rather, accept it as part of the plan of our finite lives.

Significantly, however, Jesus did not aim at his own death. He did not try to get killed. He didn't cooperate with someone else to help him die. On the contrary, when Jesus prayed in the Garden of Gethsemane, he petitioned the Father in hope that he could *avoid* death. Matthew's Gospel describes Jesus' agony in the garden:

> Then Jesus came with them to a place called Gethsemane, and he said to his disciples, "Sit here while I go over there and pray." He took along Peter and the two sons of Zebedee, and began to feel sorrow and distress. Then he said to them, "My soul is sorrowful even to death. Remain here and keep watch with me." He advanced a little and fell prostrate in prayer, saying, "My

> Father, if it is possible, let this cup pass from me; yet, not as I will, but as you will." When he returned to his disciples he found them asleep. He said to Peter, "So you could not keep watch with me for one hour? Watch and pray that you may not undergo the test. The spirit is willing, but the flesh is weak." Withdrawing a second time, he prayed again, "My Father, if it is not possible that this cup pass without my drinking it, your will be done!" Then he returned once more and found them asleep, for they could not keep their eyes open. He left them and withdrew again and prayed a third time, saying the same thing again. Then he returned to his disciples and said to them, "Are you still sleeping and taking your rest? Behold, the hour is at hand when the Son of Man is to be handed over to sinners." (26:36–45)

First, note the reference to "the final test" here, which is the same phrase used in Matthew in the Lord's Prayer (the only two times this term is used in his Gospel). Second, Jesus prays, not once but twice, that the cup might pass from him. Yet he does not entertain harmful illusions of autonomy and control (which prove so idolatrous for human beings); instead, he makes it clear that he will follow his Father's will. Jesus' death, to use phrases central to Catholic moral theology, is *foreseen* but it is *not intended*. Jesus does not extend his life at any cost, nor does he aim at his own death. In this way, he gives us an example to imitate when it comes to thinking about how our own deaths should respect human dignity.

Recall the importance of a supportive, real, embodied community on multiple levels of need (material, social, spiritual) for those who are dying. As Jesus drew closer and closer to death, it was clear that he wanted the supportive community of his inner circle of disciples. He asked them to sit with him as he made his final prayers, and he was clearly annoyed that they could not stay awake with him. Unfortunately, we learn that when Jesus was arrested and facing death, most of this inner circle fled and left him to face his death alone.

Exceptions include Mary, his mother, and John, the beloved disciple, both of whom stood at the foot of the cross as Jesus died. (Significantly, especially for topics we will engage later in this book, their exchanges were focused on getting relationships and support for after Jesus died.) This required not only courage — John was undoubtedly at risk as part of Jesus' inner circle — but steadfast compassion as well. It must have been horrific for Mary and John to stand before the cross and watch Jesus' torturous death, but they insisted that Jesus not face death without the support of his family and close friends.

Even as Jesus followed the way of the cross to his death (which Catholics follow every time they pray the Stations of the Cross), folks were willing to show him true compassion by suffering with him along the way. Jesus' mother, Mary, was there, meeting him along the path. Simon of Cyrene was there to help Jesus carry his cross. And Veronica was there to wipe his bloody and sweaty face. Though these helpers did not see their care for Jesus at this time as a burden, it does not mean it was easy or without suffering. Again, true compassion for the dying means suffering with them.

At the very end, Jesus commended his spirit into the hands of his heavenly Father, indicating the final hope we also have for after our death — a hope to be united with that same heavenly Father, whom we will finally see face-to-face. Though death is an evil, something that, in a certain sense, is rightly feared and resisted, it is also how we come to our ultimate end, our ultimate destiny. Jesus' death is bookended, of course, by the Resurrection, which indicates that death has been defanged and defeated. Death has lost its ultimate sting. Jesus came to destroy the hold death has on us. With his life and death clearly in front of our minds, we can live and die in faith.

Listening to the Voice of Jesus Today

Jesus tells us that he comes to us today in multiple special and intimate ways. Whenever "two or three are gathered together in my name," Jesus says, "there am I in the midst of them" (Mt 18:20). Of course, Jesus also tells us that he is really and truly present in the Eucharist, when the bread and wine become the "true food" of his flesh and the "true drink" of his blood (Jn 6:55). A third way in which Jesus comes to us (perhaps the most common way, especially relative to how often we acknowledge it) is through our encounters with the least among us.

Recall that, as Christians, we are called to look at the world through a lens that sees the least ones, those who are most vulnerable, as bearing the Holy Face of Christ in a special way and therefore as populations that deserve special priority. And this priority consists not only in caring for their needs but also in listening to the holiness and wisdom they have to offer us. Not every single vulnerable person is right about every single matter, of course, but to the extent that these populations speak overall and in the main with a collective voice, we should listen quite carefully.

Note that we've already seen some of what vulnerable populations think about death and dying in relation to physician-assisted killing, and we should remember that these populations offer us the holiness and wisdom of Christ. We saw in some detail how disabled communities have resisted PAK. We saw that Native and First Nations people are also disproportionately opposed to it. Something similar is true of economically vulnerable peoples. Black Americans also fall into the opposition camp, and it is worth pausing to offer a bit more detail on this.

Black Americans have a particular and long-standing skepticism when it comes to the U.S. health-care system in general and to end-of-life practices in particular.[3] The history of medical racism in the United States is a terrible evil.[4] Significant attention has been paid in recent years to the Tuskegee syphilis trials (in which, among other things, none of the hundreds of men who participated were told of their diagnosis). Less well known, however, is the fact that, in medical schools, both free and enslaved Blacks have been used without consent to help teach anatomy. The graves of Blacks have been robbed and their bodies exhumed to use as educational cadavers. Blacks were also used in radical surgical experiments.[5]

Perhaps it is this context that helps explain a particular skepticism among Black Americans when it comes to the end of life. When Pew asked whether "there are circumstances in which a patient should be allowed to die" or "medical staff should do everything possible to save a patient's life in all circumstances," a striking racial gap revealed itself.[6] For Whites, only 20 percent say everything possible should be done, but for Blacks, that number is 52 percent. Distrust of the medical system that serves them at the end of life is so profound among Blacks that it even leads to skepticism of hospice — something that, for most White families, is close to an unquestioned good.[7]

Given all this history and data, it is unsurprising that Pew finds that Black populations are far more skeptical of PAK than are Whites.[8] And this is borne out quite dramatically in the data. A twenty-three-year study found that, astonishingly, 95.6 percent of those who died by PAK were White.[9] In 2023, Oregon saw 367 people die by PAK, and only two were Black.[10] Lest one think this is simply about Oregon being an overwhelmingly White state (which, given what we have just seen, makes it anything but surprising that it was the first state to legalize PAK), something similar exists in New Jersey. This racially diverse state has had legalized PAK since 2019, but the first Black person to use it didn't do so until 2023.

Recall that those populations who are broadly in support of PAK are not only overwhelmingly White, but able-bodied and economically and socially privileged. Unlike populations that bear the Face of Christ in a special way, they tend to emphasize the myths of the autonomy and power of the individual as master of his or her life. They tend to be very highly educated and disproportionately occupy relatively powerful places in our culture. But the Gospel proclaimed by Jesus Christ turns this perspective on its head. Those who have power and wealth are the ones who have their salvation most immediately at risk, while the holiness and wisdom of Christ himself shines through the least among us. With these insights in mind, it becomes quite easy to "do the math" on which voices to privilege and which demand our skepticism when it comes to PAK. In following Christ, we listen carefully to the least among us and are skeptical of the perspectives shared by the powerful and the privileged.

CHAPTER THREE

Three Catholic Saints on Dying Well

The argument of this book would be far less powerful if it didn't take significant time to explore the resources and gifts offered by the great cloud of witnesses, the saints, the holy ones the Church of Christ has declared to be in heaven. The problem is that in a book and chapter of this length, there must be rather difficult choices made about who gets included and who gets left out. Happily, I have been able to "cheat" and add an extra saint by engaging the life and thoughts of St. Francis of Assisi in the next chapter, which focuses specifically on monks and friars. In this chapter, we will engage three saints: Joseph, Teresa of Ávila, and Robert Bellarmine.

Saint Joseph

A bit over 150 years ago, Saint Joseph, the foster father of Jesus, was declared Patron of the Universal Church by Blessed Pius IX. Pope Francis used the 150th anniversary of that pronouncement to declare a year dedicated to St. Joseph (from December 8, 2020, to December 8, 2021) and also released an apostolic letter honoring the great saint.[1] In this relatively brief document, the word *protect* is used no fewer than thirteen times. Saint Joseph understood the dignity of the human person and his duty, particularly as a man (betrothed and married to Mary and father to Jesus), to protect vulnerable human beings. He is obviously well known for moving his family in the middle of the night, fleeing to Egypt so as to avoid the wrath of King Herod and the slaughter of the Holy Innocents (every boy in the vicinity of Bethlehem under two years old). Even when Mary became pregnant before they had consummated their marriage, and Joseph had every reason to publicly declare his victimization by her supposed unfaithfulness, he instead decided to protect Mary by choosing to separate from her quietly and privately. Or consider the descriptors of Joseph in his great litany: "faithful guardian of Christ," "protector of the Church," "guardian of the Virgin," and the like. In the words of Pope Francis, Saint Joseph is "courageously and firmly proactive" in his protection of human dignity.[2]

Saint Joseph also understood and lived out the truth that human beings are finite, dependent creatures who should harbor no illusions that we are the ones who are ultimately, autonomously in charge of our lives. Saints generally have an outstanding prominence-to-humility ratio, but the foster father of the Son of God has to be among the best of them all. The paucity of stories about him in Sacred Scripture suggests that Joseph was willing to fade into the background, into the shadows. According to John Cavadini, what we do get from him in Scripture (especially in the Gospel of Matthew) evokes "an image of a man with a rich interior life, intent on doing God's will, always on the lookout for indications of his will, and ready to obey."[3] Whatever the opposite of "all about him" is, that's Saint Joseph.

He obeyed even when God's will seemed extremely odd, countercultural, or life changing. In response to the angel who delivered God's message that he was to take as his wife a woman who was pregnant by the Holy Spirit, he obeyed. In response to the angel who told him to uproot his family and relocate them to Egypt for an undetermined amount of time, he obeyed. Two other times (that we know of) an angel gave Joseph direction from God, and Joseph obeyed. He clearly taught Jesus to obey his parents (see Lk 2:51) and, of course, to do the will of his heavenly Father. No wonder one of the key monikers in his litany is "Joseph most obedient."

Saint Joseph's obedience was not without its difficulties and even, no doubt, significant sufferings. But his compassion for Mary and Jesus drove him to take on these duties of a husband and father regardless. Taking Mary as his wife, already pregnant, in an extremely unusual family situation, must have been profoundly unsettling. Setting up shop for his family in a foreign land such as Egypt must have also been extremely difficult. And, again, his significant labors and sacrifices for his family led to no claims of fame and glory for himself. For, as Cavadini notes, "Saint Joseph's identity is completely coincident with his roles as husband and father, without remainder."

And yet his willingness to put aside his will and set God's will as primary in his life is what makes Joseph's life so holy, so saintly. The devil is on the lookout to exploit claims to high status, to pomp, to self-promotion and the illusions that go along with these things — illusions that become occasions of pride, which opens human beings to temptation and sin. Joseph's life was characterized not by any of these illusions but, rather, by a profound sense of himself as subordinate to the will of God.

Thus, he was virtually impervious to the snares and temptations of Satan.

Because he lived God's will his whole life, there's little doubt that Saint Joseph's death was also characterized by the strength to accept God's will in the face of difficulties. The Scriptures are silent about Joseph after Jesus was twelve years old, but the tradition of the Church is that Joseph died well before Jesus started his public ministry. Tradition also suggests an unusually close relationship between Jesus and his foster father. Cavadini cites a beautiful example in a mosaic of Saint Joseph commissioned by Pope St. John XXIII and placed over the side altar in St. Peter's Basilica, where the Blessed Sacrament is reserved. In the mosaic, Joseph is holding the toddler Jesus in his right arm. Joseph is looking at the person beholding the mosaic, but Jesus, Cavadini notes, pays no attention to anything else besides being "wholly delighted with his dad."

What would it have meant for Jesus, so delighted by a father who taught him so much (including his profession as a carpenter), to lose his father at a young age? If Jesus' reaction to the death of Lazarus is any indication, he probably learned to "snort in spirit" in the face of death's profound evil. But he also probably learned from Joseph how to see dying and death as a final and great submission to the will and plan of God for our lives — and as a bridge to a fuller union with our heavenly Father. It is likely that the dying and death of Joseph had a significant impact on the gifts Christ would offer the Church through the Sacraments of Anointing of the Sick and Viaticum, the Eucharist given to the dying as food for the journey into eternal life. Jesus saw up close the need human beings have to experience him as an intimate travel partner for such a journey.

Recall the paradox that forms the central tension at the heart of this book: Death is rightly resisted in some contexts as a great evil, but it is also something that gives our lives meaning and can even be understood as a gift from God. With this in mind, it is important to mention that Saint Joseph is known as the patron of those who desire a "happy death." And, without doubt, he plays this role in the spiritual and prayer life of the Church because he was surrounded by the Son of God and the Mother of God at the hour of his death.

Indeed, many prayers invoke the intercession of Saint Joseph for a happy death for oneself or others. Here is one published by the Oblates of St. Joseph:

> *O Glorious St. Joseph*, I choose you today for my special patron in life and at the hour of my death. Preserve and increase in me the spirit of prayer and fervor in the service of God. Remove far from me every kind of sin; obtain for me that my death may not come upon me unawares, but that I may have time to confess my sins sacramentally and to bewail them with a most perfect understanding and a most sincere and perfect contrition, in order that I may breathe forth my soul into the hands of Jesus and Mary. Amen.[4]

St. Teresa of Ávila

A Doctor of the Church; a Carmelite nun; the recruiter and close friend of St. John of Cross; one of the most important saints of all time: This is St. Teresa of Ávila. In particular, her writings on and example of Christian mysticism and meditation are without parallel in the history of Christianity. She was canonized in 1622, only forty years after her death, and she remains a saint of very popular devotion around the world.

Her writings on death — and, in particular, her focus on the importance of "mystical death" — has been extremely influential. Again, both her writings and her own example loom large here. This book is particularly interested, as we have seen, in the central importance of supportive, real, embodied communities — and this is precisely the kind of community Saint Teresa built up through the Discalced Carmelite Order, which she cofounded with St. John of the Cross. The next chapter will focus on examples of communities provided by friars and monks, but it is worth noting here the beautiful story of Saint Teresa's refusing to die until she was joined by her younger founding partner.[5] Indeed, until his visit, she had barely the strength to breathe and her facial features were filled with tension. But upon seeing St. John of the Cross, her whole visage was filled with joy. This is yet another example of the profound importance of community and accompaniment through the dying process.

But Saint Teresa is also clear that dying well is related to living well, and vice versa. Indeed, one of her most famous quotes is deeply connected to the idea that keeping our death front of mind fundamentally shapes how we live, both in this life and with an eye to the next: "Remember that you have only one soul; that you have only one death to die; that you have only one life, which is short and has to be lived by you alone; and there is only one Glory, which is eternal. If you do this, there will be many things about which you care nothing."

Yet Saint Teresa knows that it is one thing to say this and even to believe it — and quite another to live it out. Especially in a death-denying, consumerist culture like ours, it can be quite difficult to get to the place where we "care nothing" for the idols of our age. It turns out that spiritual energies and even transformations are important for achieving our goals for living and dying well.

The central idea that Saint Teresa offers us in this context is that of a "mystical death."[6] All the great saints are grounded in the example of Christ and Sacred Scripture. We have already seen how Christ himself speaks of dying to the world and dying to the self, which makes an idol of the values of the world. But particularly important for Saint Teresa were the words and example of Saint Paul, who insists over and over that we must experience a kind of mystical death and become a new creature in Christ. In Ephesians 4, for instance, Paul says, "[You were taught to] put away the old self of your former way of life, corrupted through deceitful desires, and be renewed in the spirit of your minds, and put on the new self, created in God's way in righteousness and holiness of truth" (vv. 22–24).

Saint Teresa insists that this means, in particular, dying to self-centeredness and being reborn as a new creature focused on others. We've seen from the examples of Christ and Saint Joseph some details about what this looks like, but Saint Teresa reminds us of the power of spirituality to help bring about this transformation. Obviously, the sanctifying grace offered by baptism and other sacraments plays a key role here, but — as Teresa's life itself demonstrates — we must be ready to let the power of the Holy Spirit enter and transform our lives in unexpected and even counterintuitive ways. Indeed, both of the major spiritual turning points for Teresa in this regard came from her being very seriously ill.

The first circumstance occurred when, at age sixteen, she was discerning becoming a nun. Initially, she came to the conclusion that this kind of life was not for her. Soon after this, she developed very weak health, including regular fainting and fevers. Only with the benefit of hindsight could she look back at these experiences and see them as conduits of God's grace, leading her to a gradual submission to the kind of other-centered life to which God was calling her. Indeed, she described the transformation as akin to the one that happens to a caterpillar that turns into a butterfly.

This radical transformation in her life was completed (though she said that this transformation is something that must be renewed throughout our lives) via a second major circumstance when she was twenty. Her father had just lost his wife (her mother) and wanted Teresa to stay home and take care of the household. She loved her father very much; nevertheless, she made the decision to leave for the Carmelites — and it seems that a combination of guilt over this and the massive shift in her life circumstances led to a truly terrible illness. Indeed, she got so sick that on August 15, 1537, she had a seizure that left her unconscious for nearly four days. Everyone thought she was dying. Saint Teresa says that her convent community had dug a grave and offered her the last rites. Some even wanted to bury her, but her father insisted that she was not dead. And indeed, she regained consciousness on August 19.

As she was balancing between life and death during this time, God was giving her a transcendent experience "exceeding time and space,"[7] and it was a clear turning point for her: The death of the old happened so that the new might grow. Gone for Saint Teresa were the all-too-common human illusions of autonomy and control. But she needed to become a new kind of creature in order to see this and live it out.

St. Robert Bellarmine

St. Robert Bellarmine, the great cardinal and professor of theology, was influential in the Counter-Reformation and the Council of Trent. You may know him as an interlocutor with Galileo: Bellarmine, while deeply committed to scientific inquiry and open to new findings, engaged Galileo in debate and pointed out that the astronomer had not proven his case. (Though, true to the Church's valuing of science, Bellarmine declared that the Church would have to change her interpretation of Sacred Scripture if Galileo ever did prove his claims.)[8] Also a Doctor of the Church, Bellarmine wrote a great book titled *The Art of Dying Well*, which is an important classic for us to engage here, especially since it expands on several topics we've already explored.[9]

Given the book's title, one would, of course, not be surprised to find the author focused on death not merely as an evil or bad thing but also, in some ways, as a good thing. Bellarmine is unafraid to inhabit this complex and even tension-filled place. God did not make death (it was through human sin that death entered the world, after all), but it is also the case that, through the grace of God, "many blessings arise" from the fact of our deaths. This is true not just with obvious examples, such as the death of Jesus, but even with our own deaths, which, as we have seen, can and often do center us on what it is important in life. Indeed, Bellarmine specifically suggests that, though we need to give due consideration to the mundane affairs of daily life, we must be on guard to ensure that they do not so occupy our minds that we fail to direct "our first thoughts" toward Christ.

The first chapter in *The Art of Dying Well* is titled "He who desires to die well, must live well." Dying, rightly understood, is the last phase of our lives and thus flows from our broader choices about how to live. More will be said later about the specifics of living well in this context, but here let us mention that Bellarmine insists that we keep our death front of mind so that it can shape how we live. Like the faithful servant, we need to be on watch for the coming of the Lord. Far from being something we choose to control ourselves, "nothing is more uncertain" than the hour of our deaths.[10]

And in what does our watching consist? Bellarmine thinks that regularly reminding ourselves of the bare fact of our coming death is important, but not in a morbid, obsessive way. Indeed, he says that nothing is more useful for watching in preparation for a good death than for us to "frequently and seriously examine our conscience." The great Doctor of the Church notes that this is fairly common for those who begin to enter the dying process and even for those who are growing older and can see the end of their lives on the horizon, but he is particularly worried about those "who are snatched away by a sudden death" or "who are afflicted with madness, or fall into delirium" or who, "being grievously afflicted by their disease, cannot even think of their sins."[11]

Beyond getting right with the Lord is the duty to live well in the first place, and a central idea for Bellarmine builds on the insights of Saint Teresa. Dying to ourselves means, more specifically, dying to the logic and values of the world, which is the focus of Bellarmine's second chapter. Of course, the time, country, and other social contexts into which one is born shape what is meant by "the world" for any given person, but in every context, there is the profound risk of living as if the logic and values of the world are a kind of second (or even primary) god for us. This may also involve imagining *ourselves* as a kind of god, especially if we demand the sense of autonomy and control with which the developed world of our own time is obsessed. Such a foundational mistake leads to many bad things. We've already seen how it can lead both to fighting for extended life at any cost and to taking death into one's own hands. Those who die to our own culture must (again) die to the harmful illusion of Western-style autonomy and control.

Such harmful illusions have also led to a kind of consumerist individualism that can harm our sense of solidarity with the poor and the vulnerable. Recall the need to focus on a counterculture of encounter and hospitality and always to look through a lens that gives special priority to the least among us. But Bellarmine is explicit about the need to die to the world governed by what he called "the deceitful error of the rich." Indeed, he says that it "is necessary above all things, if we wish to be saved and to die a good death, diligently to enquire, either by our own reading and meditation, or by consulting holy and learned men, whether our 'superfluous' riches can be retained without sin, or whether we ought of necessity to give them to the poor."[12]

This also takes a really significant examination of conscience, particularly when it comes to idolatry. Bellarmine reminds us:

"You cannot serve both God and mammon." If we have wealth, are we putting it at the service of the Gospel? Of the poor, who bear the Holy Face of Christ as the least among us? Bellarmine invokes the Church Fathers and quotes their hardcore instructions in this regard: Basil, Ambrose, Jerome, John Chrysostom, Augustine, and Leo all speak of this in some way. You owe your superfluous wealth to the poor, and *you are a robber or a thief if you keep it for yourself*. God will demand an accounting of how we used the goods he entrusted to our care, and we must not be caught storing up our wealth in bigger and better barns on the night our lives come to an end.[13]

Mammon rules this world, however, and dying to this world — for most of us — requires regular reminders and examinations of conscience. That's why Bellarmine says:

> Let it, therefore, be a fixed rule for living well and dying well, often to consider and seriously to ponder on the account that must be given to God of our luxury in palaces, in gardens, in chariots, in the multitude of servants, in the splendor of dress, in banquets, in hoarding up riches, in unnecessary expenses, which injure a great multitude of the poor and sick, who stand in need of our superfluities; and who now cry to God, and in the day of judgment will not cease crying out until we, together with the rich man, shall be condemned to eternal flames.[14]

Sobering words. For many reading these words, I suspect, giving in the way that Our Lord and the great Fathers of the Church insist that we must is a big ask, and we may sinfully fail at this and serve mammon above the Living God, whose Holy Face, again, comes to us through encounters with the poor and the otherwise vulnerable. We've seen how Saint Teresa insists on the need for spiritual transformation in this regard. Bellarmine adds the importance of the Church's embodied, supportive, real community to facilitate this transformation. In particular — and this is how he closes his book — he is focused on the Sacrament of Extreme Unction, more commonly known today as anointing of the sick.

It is a time to get right with God: As Bellarmine notes, the person is connected with the priest, who offers the sacrament as he anoints the person's body and assures him or her of God's forgiveness for sins committed via those means. The sacrament also gives the person strength and courage through God's grace to endure his or her illness (one does not have to be dying to receive the sacrament) and remain on the path leading to eternal life if death is what is coming. Among other things, the sacrament connects a person to the community of those who have gone before him or her in suffering illness and death: from Christ, to the saints, to our Catholic family members whose voices and examples echo throughout the generations. The Church as a whole is close to the person receiving this sacrament. Indeed, the *Catechism of the Catholic Church* says that the communion of saints intercedes for the benefit of the sick or dying person (1522).

What a beautiful community the Church offers us as we endeavor to live well and prepare to die well. But nobody experiences community quite like Catholic monks and friars. And it is to their specific example we will now turn.

CHAPTER FOUR
The Example of Catholic Monks and Friars

It was the summer of 2023, and the novices of the Franciscan Friars of the Renewal at their friary in one of the poorest areas of Newark, New Jersey, were taking a moral theology course and learning about some of the central ideas engaged by this book. Upon learning the primary reasons people request physician-assisted killing (loss of autonomy, loss of enjoyable activities, being a burden on others, etc.), these novice friars realized that they were living lives that — by these deformed standards — would be considered good candidates for being ended via PAK.

Yet each of these men was full of love and joy. They had died to their previous selves, giving up the illusion of autonomy, giving up many of what had been their previously enjoyable activities, and sharing their needs and burdens with their brothers who provided for them in community. Their new selves, born of the Spirit, were not despairing of life; rather, they radiated the joy of self-denying Christian love that embraced the cross.

This is yet another reminder that the challenge to PAK is not centrally about how to die. Rather, it is primarily about how to live. And once again, the Christian tradition offers us essential resources in this regard by giving us the gift of the example of the vowed religious. Though later in the book we will learn from the example of women, in this chapter, we will focus on a great Catholic saint who was also perhaps the paradigmatic Christian friar: St. Francis of Assisi. Next, we will examine the *Ars Moriendi*, a classic text on the "art of dying," probably written by a fifteenth-century Dominican friar. Finally, we will examine more stories from monks and friars of the contemporary period, which point us toward the best practices for how to live in resistance to a culture slouching toward PAK.

St. Francis of Assisi

What can one say about St. Francis of Assisi? The great saint and friar holds such a special place in the hearts of Catholics and the lore of the Church that it was even somewhat shocking to many that Pope Francis would take his name. Such a standard is difficult to be associated with, to say nothing of actually living up to the saint's life of holiness! Many know of his founding of the Franciscan Order, his profound commitment to peace and to the poor, and his care for creation and animals. But the great saint has also given us one of the most provocative and helpful understandings of death in our tradition.

It didn't necessarily start out that way, however. In fact, Francis spent much of his life articulating an understanding of death that, while not mistaken, was largely unremarkable. Indeed, during this period of his life, he understood death primarily as something bad.[1] In both his early and later exhortations, Francis is concerned (again, not without reason) about the fact that death is to be feared — especially if one has been captured by the world's vanities. Mortally sinful lives snatched away by death, he says, are headed for a horrific afterlife of anguish and distress. Another important theme of this book is that we must consistently keep our own death front of mind, such that it fundamentally shapes how we live — both in this life and with an eye to the next. Francis obviously lived this out and taught this to everyone, but he has especially difficult warnings about death for the powerful of his day. In a letter to political leaders and rulers of people, he wrote:

> Reflect and see that the day of death is approaching. With all possible respect, therefore, I beg you not to forget the Lord because of the world's cares and preoccupations and not to turn away from his commandments, for those who leave him in oblivion and turn away from his commandments are cursed and will be left in oblivion by him. When the day of death does come, everything they have will be taken from them.[2]

So, yeah, death is scary and bad, especially for the most privileged. This is certainly one side of the coin. But over the course of his life, Francis's views on these matters would grow and mature, achieving their full and nuanced flowering as Francis approached his own death. It was then he would boldly and famously name death "Sister." This naming comes in the context of his writing the well-known "Canticle of the Creatures"[3] (out of which Pope Francis took the name of his great encyclical *Laudato Si'*, or "Praised Be You [Lord]"). The canticle was created over several years and would not receive its final form until the saint was on his deathbed. Many readers will be familiar with the first section, in which Saint Francis praises his heavenly Father for the gift of creation, naming the sun, the moon, the earth, and the like as siblings. The second section focuses on peace and reconciliation. The third and final part of the canticle is of the most interest to us, as it contains the remarkable line: "Praised be You, my Lord, through our Sister Bodily Death, from whom no one living can escape."

What a remarkable and radical image! How could someone go from seeing death as something bad and to be feared to this much more nuanced place? To seeing the visit of death as the visit of a sibling? Author Daniel Horan thinks that it is Francis's connection to all of creation and to peacemaking that leads to the kind of self-emptying that allows him to move from seeing death as totally alien and merely to be feared to seeing it as another dimension of who we are. Death is another entity with whom we have a relationship, and through that relationship, it helps us discover ourselves. And this makes a good deal of sense. A central idea in this book is that we must embrace our interdependence and relationships, rejecting the harmful illusions of individual autonomy and control. Saint Francis's growing realization of our radical connection to and dependence on God's broader creation helped him do precisely this.

Others, like Mary Petrosky, a Franciscan Missionary of Mary, believe that Saint Francis's transformation was the result of spiritual experiences he had while on retreat at Mount La Verna — a retreat during which he was mystically transformed into the dying Christ and was given the gift of the stigmata. Petrosky notes that Francis had been unsuccessfully seeking a traditional martyrdom throughout his life but was instead given this kind of little death — a death to self that allowed him to give himself fully to Christ.[4] God led him away from a life in which he was *seeking* his own death (seemingly and dangerously close to aiming at his own death) to a life in which he could *welcome* death as a sister when it came, without actively seeking it. This obviously has important resonances with central themes of this book.

Another central theme of this book is that, in both living and dying, the central importance of a supportive, real, embodied community is ridiculously important. This is true on multiple levels of need — material, social, spiritual — and it allows the community to suffer with the sufferer. Such compassionate care is an opportunity to love, not merely a burden. As we will see below, communities of monks and friars do this very well — and the religious community Francis created was no exception.

Indeed, according to David Torkington, the relationships Francis had developed over the course of his life were rekindled in new and dramatic ways, especially as he went to meet the Lord.[5] He was infirm and unable to do much for himself, but with the approach of Sister Death, Francis asked his brothers to take him to the little church he had built: St. Mary of the Angels. There he was to be placed in a tiny, simple hut. Ever mindful of the central lens and value of his life, Francis wanted to die as he had lived: loving "Lady Poverty" until the end. He wanted nothing approaching ostentatious ritual or gifts or the like, even asking that he be placed in the ground with no coffin, without even the modest covering of his Franciscan habit.

There was apparently a long procession in which, among other things, his brothers raised him up so he could look about his hometown of Assisi (and so many of its important landmarks) for the last time. Once on his bed in his hut, steps from church, he had many important encounters, including ones in which he gave forgiveness to those who asked for it. He gave special blessings to those who were important in his life. Old friends showed up from far away to recall old times and pay their respects. Francis begged his especially close friends to remain close to him as death approached. As his earthly journey came to an end, he reenacted the Last Supper with his brothers, taking bread and sharing it with those around him — all while

Scripture passages were read. After Sister Death arrived, the silence was broken only by a flock of larks (Saint Francis's favorite bird) that descended on his hut.

The *Ars Moriendi*

Perhaps the paradigmatic Catholic source for the art of dying well is the *Ars Moriendi*. Written by an unknown friar (probably a Dominican) in the fifteenth century, it became wildly popular and widely read in Christian Europe. It certainly didn't hurt that it was written in the context of the major Council of Constance, which charged the Dominicans and Franciscans with its dissemination.[6] Also important was the invention of the printing press and the fact that, in many cases, the text was accompanied by illustrations (and even engravings) to help semiliterate people understand what was being taught.

In this sense, the authors and disseminators of the *Ars Moriendi* were deeply concerned about giving special priority to the most vulnerable, the least ones of the day. Indeed, the idea was to make sure that those on the margins who didn't really have access to priests or the sacraments would be spiritually instructed and strengthened when it came to matters of life and death. In this way, the document was beautifully non-elitest. Indeed, by analogy, it may be helpful to think about it as a kind of self-help literature of the fifteenth century. Meant to be read when one was in relatively good health, the *Ars* instructs readers primarily about how to think about something we've addressed here many times: the relationship between a good life and a good death.

Why would so many people at that time be without access to priests and the sacraments? The main reason is that Christian Europe in the fifteenth century was just coming out of the massive upheaval of the Black Death, during which perhaps 50 percent of the population had died. Add to that the first stages of the bloodbath of the Hundred Years' War, and you've got the kind of cultural disruption in which the Church's structures simply couldn't function as they otherwise would. Unlike in our time, obviously, there was no need to remind people that we must consistently keep death front of mind. Death was ubiquitous in this moment in history, and everyone was thinking about it, pretty much all the time. Indeed, Allen Verhey suggests that death was so present that it focused the people of this era in such a way that they became uniquely preoccupied with their individual selves — and with keeping themselves from dying like so many others around them.[7]

The *Ars Moriendi* pushed back on this cultural shift in a fundamental way: It insisted that the person contemplating his or her own death must step outside of any self-obsession, particularly by understanding, as Stephen Doran says, that the death of the soul is immeasurably worse than the death of the body.[8] The *Ars* insists that the devil's strategy is to turn people away from their faith in despair. Reassuringly, in the *Ars*, the illustration of this temptation indicates that many spiritual warriors stand ready to help strengthen the faith of the person challenged by death. Angels; Mary, the Mother of God; Moses; many saints; and even Jesus and God the Father are lined up by the dying person's bed, ready to help. The Holy Spirit, in the image of the dove, flies across the dying man's headboard.

One of the key principles we have repeated many times in this book is that human beings are inherently finite, dependent, and social creatures; this means that we must reject the harmful illusion that we are autonomous individuals who can somehow overcome our proper place in the created order. This misunderstanding leads to the idolatrous extremes of fighting for extended life at any cost or responding to dying by taking death into one's own hands. The *Ars* is concerned about these matters as they show up in the temptations to pride and impatience. In describing the illustration of the temptation to impatience, Verhey notes that a single demon seems to be doing a very good job here, as the dying man is lashing out in his frustration, even kicking the physician away from the bed and knocking over the side table. In a subsequent image, the defeat of the temptation to impatience is shown with the dying man serenely at prayer. He is surrounded by angels and the great martyrs, including Saint Stephen holding the stones that killed him. Christ is there as well, bearing his crown of thorns and a scourge. A great multitude, in spiritual support, stand ready to share in this man's suffering.

Interestingly, the *Ars* warns the reader against the temptation to avarice, thus reminding us of the need to give special priority to the most vulnerable, especially the poor. The demon in the illustration asks the dying man to focus on his treasures. This is understood not just as attachment to gold and other riches but as attachment to all temporal things of this world — a kind of holding on to the things the world values rather than what is of God and the good of returning to God. But once again, this illustration shows the mighty powers of resistance: Christ on his cross, fully emptying himself; Mary, who gave her only Son over to torment and death; and angels, reminding the dying man to hold on to God and not his treasures.

As I've mentioned several times now, it is difficult to overemphasize the central importance of a supportive community in this context. Yes, we have a dramatic spiritual community at the ready to help, as illustrated in the *Ars*, but the *Ars* is also absolutely clear about the need for a local, embodied community of support to be present. And there should be some mutual back-and-forth between the dying person and the community. The person facing death should reach out and reconcile with neighbors, friends, and family. And the community much reach back with their support — but also with important reminders about being reconciled to God, offering no false hope for the person dying. Indeed, in the fifteenth century, even those who didn't know the dying person well were encouraged to get in on the act. "Dying in the fifteenth century," Lydia Dugdale notes, "was truly a communal affair."[9] Beyond this, though, the *Ars* takes care to emphasize that the person facing death should have the support of a single faithful and suitable friend to be a special partner throughout the process.

Finally, we know the importance of the following distinction: We should resist death when appropriate but should also discern the time to accept and even welcome (but not aim at or choose) death as a gift from God. This is something that the *Ars* emphasizes as well. Yes, though spiritual death is worse, physical death is obviously understood to be a bad thing. And yet, once again, we have a tension, emphasized by Psalm 116:15 and Revelation 14:13: "Precious in the sight of the Lord is the death of his faithful ones" (NRSV) and "Blessed are the dead who die in the Lord." Ecclesiastes 7:1 tells us that the day of death is better than the day of birth. And we also read in Saint Paul's Letter to the Philippians: "I long to depart this life and be with Christ, [for] that is far better" (1:23). As Saint Francis taught in his life, we are called to welcome death as a beloved and trusted friend.

An Example from Our Own Time

In a unique 2019 book titled *A Time to Die: Monks on the Threshold of Eternal Life*, French author Nicholas Diat offers us the fruit of his important labors: interviews with monks in eight European monasteries.[10] The stories are simply extraordinary, especially as they build on the long-established tradition of those who had gone before them.

Diat opens with a description of a Capuchin crypt in Rome, with five chapels adorned, floor to ceiling, "with the bones of the monks of ages past." On the wooden placard greeting visitors is a warning: "We were like you; you will be like us."[11] Diat notes that we in the developed West have had to work hard to undermine a culture that gave us such warnings as a matter of course, but undermine it we have. We no longer know how to die, and fear and anxiety rule the day.

Thus, Diat says, he had the idea to go to the great monasteries in order "to discover what the monks might teach us about death."[12] What he found there was hope: hope that contemporary humanity can die humanely. We are not condemned to die alone in hospital rooms, nor are we forced to engage death in the false image created by funeral parlors. Instead, the monks Diat engaged spoke to him of "the radiant, peaceful, and luminous deaths of the friends of God."[13] Were these deaths so peaceful because of the heroic virtues of monks who never had fears, sorrows, and torments? On the contrary, the monks experienced all of these. What was different was how the community prepared them for dying by the way they lived their lives, and how they rallied around them in their final journey to the Lord.

Take, for example, Diat's experience at the abbey of the Canons Regular of the Mother of God in the village of Lagrasse, France. The abbey was home to thirty-five relatively young Augustinians, many of whom had, by the world's standards, prestigious careers ahead of them before they signed up for a very different kind of life. Among those who chose this very different kind of life was Br. Vincent Marie, a thirty-six-year-old who suffered badly from multiple sclerosis — so badly, in fact, that Diat discovered that a grave had already been dug for him. Diat's reaction was one of anger over such an early and difficult death — coupled with questions: Did Brother Vincent fear death? Was he fighting for more life in the face of what seemed like a done deal?

Diat got to know the history of the young friar. Brother Vincent, much like what we saw with Saint Teresa in the previous chapter, interpreted his illness as an invitation from God to live out the vocation that he had rejected as a younger man —

though, as he took his first vows, the illness really began to hit: such significant shaking in his right hand that he was forced to become left-handed. Not long after that, his left hand also began to shake, and he was forced to give up his particular expertise: restoring and maintaining the abbey as an electrician. He became so generous and collegial in sharing his expertise, however, that his brothers were able to take over his work.

His brother monks noted that this was a significant change in his life. His illness and commitment to his new vocation, apparently, dramatically changed a man who had had problems with egoism, fear, and selfishness. Early on, as the brothers lived two to a room without heating, Brother Vincent had gotten off to a rough start. But the community's firm commitment to one another and to their traditions and rules brought real spiritual growth. Especially in light of such growth, there was hope that Brother Vincent would get better. He seemed to be in the process of being formed to live out many years in this community.

That was not to be, however. As Brother Vincent's legs deteriorated, he was unable to walk straight even with the help of a cane. He stumbled against walls. As it became clear that he would never walk properly again, the superiors of the abbey decided to move his room from the second floor to the first floor — in part, according to Diat, "to bring him closer to the places of community life."[14]

And it was real community life: Brother Vincent still had the energy to be a real center of attention. Even when he visited a medical center specializing in multiple sclerosis, his social passion — and his passion for evangelization — was front and center. When encountering nurses, patients, and family members, he would talk with them about the saints, give people medals, and say Rosaries. There was no time for resting. He would often be found with a couple of guests seated on the edge of his bed listening to him talk about the Faith.

As the disease progressed, however, it become more painful — and louder. Pain infiltrated every corner: the sound of a knife on a plate held by a shaking hand; a dropped book in the choir loft; multiple falls in the hallways. Diat describes the brothers as firemen always ready to put out fires related to these kinds of issues. When Brother Vincent took his final vows, someone else had to hold the candle and the ritual book. His whole body trembled. When seen by the nurses at this stage of his illness, he could no longer read. Still, as part of his attempts at evangelization, he would ask them to read him sections from great spiritual authors. In 2012, his illness got so bad that his superiors moved him out of his room and into the infirmary. Indeed, his brothers reorganized the infirmary specifically for him and his unique needs.

Once in his new digs, Brother Vincent prayed that God would take him quickly to heaven — but, mirroring the prayer of the Lord in the Garden of Gethsemane, he also prayed that God would do as he pleased. Eventually, his accompanying brothers found themselves caring for a Brother Vincent who could no longer speak coherently. They tried to help him construct sentences. They suggested responses for him. It was difficult for them to watch his sufferings, but watch them they did, even sleeping next to him on the floor when things were particularly bad for him.

Apart from these moments, the brothers got used to being awakened multiple times during the night to come to his aid. This happened especially as Brother Vincent faced multiple bouts with mucus that choked him and put his life at risk. His body had become so weak that he had to be turned over by another person to allow him to cough the mucus out. The presence of his brothers during this time was important even beyond avoiding a terrible death by suffocation. Brother Vincent could not sleep by himself, but if other religious were present, according to Diat, "he slept like a sparrow."[15]

When he could no longer talk, one of the priests of the house relayed the following encounter with Brother Vincent:

> I told him several times that he should let go. ... I encouraged him: he could depart. He knew that the canons were torn. But we were ready. I sensed that he wanted to fight. Fifteen days before his death, I asked him not to stay if his reason for living was the community's pain. Brother Vincent searched me with his big eyes, then he stared in space for a long time. Finally, he blinked to signify he had understood. I did not know what he wanted, but he had heard me. I took his hand and told him the brothers would greatly mourn his death; most importantly, it was his choice, his freedom, his decision. Deep inside, I hoped God would come for him.[16]

Diat said that Brother Vincent's suffering body itself "had become a prayer,"[17] though he himself could no longer pray. He was told that his mother was on her way to him, and he seemed to wait to die until that moment. Once she came into the room, the infirmarian sensed that Brother Vincent was about to die. Priests and brothers rushed to the room to be with him at his passing — a passing that one priest described as happening "with great ease."[18] The brother recited the prayers of the dying at his bedside, and suddenly, everyone had the sense that Brother Vincent was at peace, no longer swimming in the ocean of suffering. Just before, his face had been contorted in pain; now it was radiant. All the brothers knelt down to honor his passing into eternal life.

Then came a time for others to be transformed by his death. On the day of Brother Vincent's burial, Diat describes the "joy" that penetrated "even the stones of the abbey."[19] His grave had been dug two years earlier, but now it would be occupied and closed. The climb to the cemetery involved the whole community and wound its way through the glories of God's creation. Those in the procession walked through beautiful gardens, beheld the magnificent blue sky, and listened to the many singing birds.

Ten days after Brother Vincent's death, his intercession brought about otherwise unexplainable healings of terminally ill people. Those may have been supernatural miracles, but other kinds of miracles took place as well, particularly in the formation of the brothers who cared for their sick and dying brother. They were able to debrief about their own fears and anxieties and suffering in going through this process. No sugarcoating there. But they were also inspired and spiritually shaped by this process in ways maybe no other event could have done. Those who were close to Brother Vincent, says Diat, were transformed. "Fragile and nervous brothers became rocks."[20]

This is a significantly shortened version of only one of several stories that appear in Diat's remarkable book. But notice the key ideas and principles central to this story: Obviously, in both living and dying, the central importance of a supportive, real, embodied community (on multiple levels of need: material, social, spiritual) was present throughout. The illusions of autonomy and control were gone, and thus the twin idolatries of fighting for extended life at any cost and responding to dying by taking death into one's own hands were not serious concerns in this story. Both Brother Vincent and the community surrounding him were eager and ready to resist death when appropriate, but they were also able to discern the time to accept and even welcome death as a gift from God. And notice that Brother Vincent was able to die well because of his formation in living well. One transferred quite neatly over to the other.

Of course, this community has built-in advantages over most other communities. They have not only their explicit and ancient practices of general human and spiritual formation but also their physical spaces, the availability of brothers to serve, the resistance to our consumerist culture, and centuries-old traditions of caring for dying members of the community — something that obviously keeps death front of mind in ways that shape how the brothers live. This community is poised to face death well. And yet, as mostly young members of the community, they had to learn through practice. It was through putting this particular kind of compassionate love into practice that they themselves were transformed into the kinds of brothers they were meant to be. What may have been considered nothing more than a burden was actually an incredible gift.

CHAPTER FIVE

Care Homes and Hospices Today

We've explored a good bit of history up to this point, but this chapter will continue to draw us back to our current moment, considering especially how we care for older adults and the sick and dying in care homes and hospices. There is a lot of contemporary discussion of these matters, including in secular circles, especially after the COVID-19 pandemic revealed just how terribly we treat these populations.[1]

But before diving into some examples of our contemporary situation, it would be good to take one more look at the historical record so we can understand better the history of these institutions. I've already mentioned that the Catholic Church invented the contemporary concept of the hospital, which was created to cure patients, but it is something that grew out of a far simpler concept: homes (called hospices) that cared for the aging, the sick, and the dying as they passed into such phases of life. Going back to at least the fourth century, Christians led the way in creating these unique institutions, which proliferated all over medieval Europe, run mainly by religious orders. This kind of Christian care for the sick and the dying in these institutions became ubiquitous and was so welcome that it greatly contributed to the Church's strong influence in the Western world.[2]

Though the backlash against religious orders in Europe in the early modern period would hurt the development of the care home and hospice movement, the practice was revived by the Daughters of Charity of St. Vincent de Paul in seventeenth-century France.[3] The Irish Sisters of Charity would go on to take this work to England and many other European countries. The United States saw its first hospice opened in 1974 and explicitly used St. Christopher's Hospice in England as a model.[4]

Care homes and hospices are still operated by many religious orders, and they give us important insight into the ideas and goals animating this book. This is a fact we should not find surprising, given that they are inspired explicitly by the example and vision of those who have gone before them. In this first section of this chapter, we will focus on care homes generally, followed by sections on care for people with dementia and those who are dying and cared for in a hospice context.

Carmelite Sisters of the Most Sacred Heart of Los Angeles

We've already seen the genius of the Carmelites in these spaces, in particular through the example offered by the great Doctor of the Church St. Teresa of Ávila. But let's fast-forward to our own time, to the Carmelites of the Most Sacred Heart serving in Los Angeles in a care home named for their greatest saint: Santa Teresita. Here is the home's mission statement (keep in mind the principles we have been discussing throughout this book as you read it):

> We uphold and promote the dignity of life at all stages through quality care to those whom we serve and their families. The Carmelite Sisters and staff of Santa Teresita are dedicated to the physical, spiritual, and relational needs of each resident. We strive to provide the most homelike and supportive environment possible, empowering the lives of all with vibrancy, purpose, and fulfillment that they may thrive during their golden years. The latter years of life are meant to be rewarding, filled with purpose and nurturing.[5]

We've seen in this book several examples of caring for the full needs of human beings, but these Carmelite sisters are among the best at doing so, reflecting the fullness of the healing ministry of Jesus. They insist that their residents' lives "be overflowing with the beauty of nature, the joy of companionship, physical and social involvement, the love of family, friends, pets, and above all: a special closeness to God." Residents are offered many wonderful opportunities to grow in faith, including:

- Holy Mass
- Rosary
- Communion distribution to residents
- Pastoral Care from the Carmelite Sisters
- Access to Saint Joseph Chapel and Sacred Heart Chapel in the Medical Office Building
- Opportunities to receive the Sacrament of the Anointing of the Sick
- Bible studies
- Spiritual library including a variety of books, tapes,

and DVDs on all topics of the Catholic Faith
- Special feast day and holiday celebrations[6]

Sr. Magdalene Grace, a registered nurse who has served in eldercare for the last decade, offered a particularly dramatic example of how attention to spiritual health served one of their residents during his last moment on earth:

> I was with a resident and his family while he was actively dying and I could tell he was anxious and not at peace. Surrounding his bed, we began to pray the divine mercy chaplet. I recall interiorly begging Our Lord to restore peace in his soul before his last breath. At that moment, I heard a bell ringing which in our homes means Jesus, truly present in the Most Blessed Sacrament, was on His way! A sister came into the room with the Blessed Sacrament, knelt at the foot of the bed, and joined us in prayer. The resident's look of anxiety and panic changed into a radiant peace, and he closed his eyes and died. The entire room of people burst into tears and began rejoicing and hugging one another. I think we all knew we had witnessed "the dawn from on high break upon us" and guide his soul into the way of peace.[7]

This parallels the story of Brother Vicent's death in the previous chapter in remarkable ways. Here again, we see the importance of the presence of community and how attending to all levels of need — including spiritual need — helped turn both deaths from difficult struggles into peaceful transitions.

Sr. Cecelia Marie, also a registered nurse, emphasized a central theme of this book, insisting that it is not just a good death that resists physician-assisted killing but also a good life. In a throwaway culture that tells people their lives are good only when they are productive, independent, and autonomous, Santa Teresita offers a counterculture of encounter that shows older adults, the sick, and the dying that their lives are good for their own sakes and that it is gift to care for them:

> Some of our residents will say things like, "I'm just taking up space." Or "I didn't want to call for help because you all have a lot of other things to do." And I can't tell you how much joy it brings me to see the change in their countenance when I can express through my presence with them that they are loved and delighted in and worth my time; that their needs are the very occasion of my encounter with them, and the opportunity to receive from the richness of their lives. If we can help people to experience the love of the Sacred Heart of Jesus through the attention and presence we give them, we can combat the "throw-away" culture because no one wants to throw away what is valuable to them. And if people do not experience being valued, what is to stop them from throwing life away? It really comes down to love, because the love we experience from God is the source of our love and acceptance even of the most "burdensome" in our society.

One of the sisters' administrators of the sisters' care home in the Los Angeles area, Sr. Marie Estelle (who is also a nurse), is particularly passionate about changing the expectations our culture has developed when it comes to care homes for these populations:

> Institutional experiences of the past (i.e., the stereotypical nursing homes of long hallways, awful odors, etc.) need to be abandoned in favor of embracing a "whole life" view of the person who deserves love and care. The "Eden Al-

ternative" model founded by Dr. Bill Thomas has as its premise that no matter how much medicine and "expert" medical care elders received ... they did not thrive. He had a fascinating story of how he came to see that what plagues elders is loneliness, helplessness, and boredom. The antidote is not in medicine alone ... but in the hearts of those who practice medicine. To see with the heart, to connect with the broken spirit, to bring hope and love and connection when a culture has set them aside. Also that we were originally designed to live in a Garden (Eden) with connection to beauty, nature, and relationships.

Such care for the whole person has the benefit of taking away the fear people have as they enter these stages of life. Fear, Sister Estelle says, is what pushes many to pursue the idolatrous extremes of fighting for extended life at any cost or trying to take death into one's own hands. She and her colleagues regularly see both patterns of thinking, and they "can happen to anyone." Again, it comes back to love — a love that dispels fear, and can help people live with difficulties, and also a love that, with "gentle acceptance and peace," can help people die.

Sometimes that love can be incredibly, movingly intimate — and creative. Sister Estelle described the following example of caring for a deaf man who could not hear the gentle songs that were being sung for him as he was approaching his final days:

> I felt this incredible surge of love come into my mind and my heart for this elderly man, and I saw him as a little boy beloved of God the Father. His sister was softly singing, and I realized that he needed to receive a different way of being accompanied to know he was not alone, since he was deaf. I gently placed my arms under each of his shoulders and kind of cradled his head in my

right hand and just ever so slightly rocked him back up and down on the bed. Giving him a sense that he was "held" and not alone. In Catholic health care, we truly become God's hands and feet, instruments where God's love can *surge* through us as the Lord prepares to bring them across the threshold of eternity.

Sister Estelle also emphasized that our throwaway culture has, embedded deep within it, a sense that our needs constitute burdens on other people's individual autonomy and freedom. Interestingly, she names this problem as a kind of disordered pride — and thus names the solution as a kind of rightly ordered humility. Both giver and receiver need to put their pride aside in allowing the logic of love to replace the logic of burden.

Finally, Sister Estelle emphasized that the whole ministry, again, is focused on imitating the love Jesus had for people right up until the end:

> To look into people's eyes and love them. To hold their hands. Our Mother Foundres, Venerable Maria Luisa Josefa, taught us to: "See every room as a chapel, every bed as an altar, and ever patient as Christ." To offer solid medical care with pain management, while not stepping across the line of taking the place and timing of God's Fatherly Providence on when that last breath is to be drawn. This is the difference in a Catholic atmosphere. There are intangible graces when one is on mission for a supernatural end in mind. Our finest work is loving to the end. We love and have hope. We are not afraid of the darkness. This doesn't mean that all deaths are easy — they are not. And the grief of loss is real. As saints before would run to care for lepers, serve soldiers on the war fields, give of their riches to serve the poor, and

spend their lives in prayer, we only seek to participate in Christ's mission to heal the sick and set the captives free. We all are captives, captives to sin and destined to death. Hope in his Saving Blood and Mercy gives us the hope of a life without end. To be enveloped in Infinite love where, one day, every tear will be wiped away (Rev 21).

The Little Sisters of the Poor

The Little Sisters of the Poor! If all you've heard of them comes from stories about contraceptive mandates, or from various jokes in which they appear, draw near to this section of the chapter and read it carefully. Present in hundreds of houses in more than thirty countries, the Little Sisters follow their French foundress, St. Jeanne Jugan, who had a view of the world that gave a special priority to the poor. Indeed, she said, "Never forget that the poor are Our Lord. In caring for the poor say to yourself: This is for my Jesus — what a great grace!"[8]

Sr. Constance Veit, director of communications for the Little Sisters in the United States, offers us the following moving account of how Sister Jugan and the order she founded responded to the signs of the times:

> The Little Sisters personified the Church's preferential option for the poor and most abandoned. In the early decades of our nation's history, elders depended on their children or personal wealth to assure a comfortable old age. Poorhouses, modeled on England's "Poor Laws," sheltered the indigent elderly, but they were characterized by primitive, often subhuman conditions.
>
> By the 1850s, benevolent societies and fraternal organizations began to organize old age homes and other forms of assistance for those able to pay monthly dues while they were young so that they could receive help

in their old age. What was novel about the Little Sisters' mission was that they came to America specifically to care for those who could not pay their own way.[9]

Even more specific signs of the times to which the Little Sisters responded were the changes wrought by the Industrial Revolution (which, in the words of Sister Constance, "encouraged a utilitarian mindset that treated human workers as machines" while "those perceived as unproductive were cast aside"), particularly as those changes played out in the United States. Significantly, they came to the United States with virtually nothing and "set up shop in empty buildings, depending on the generosity of the local community to provide all that was needed for the care of the poor."[10]

The Little Sisters, to this day, are resisters of a throwaway culture that dismisses and discards the vulnerable elderly, the sick, and the dying, and they do so with a counterculture of encounter and hospitality. Indeed, they take a specific "vow of hospitality," by which they promise God to consecrate themselves

> totally to the service of the elderly poor. We serve them day and night, striving to meet their physical needs, to make them happy and to minister to them spiritually. Our lives are made up of many humble, hidden tasks. We accomplish our mission together as a community, each one bringing her gifts and talents to the work of hospitality. Continuing the work of Saint Jeanne Jugan, our mission offers the neediest elderly of every race and religion a Home where they will be welcomed as Christ, cared for as family and accompanied with dignity until God calls them to himself.[11]

A Little Sister with training in ethics at the motherhouse in

France sees this kind of hospitality as specifically resisting physician-assisted killing and euthanasia. Laws permitting such practices, because they "respect neither the life nor the dignity of the person," actually push and "provoke" the sisters "to offer spaces where life is promoted, defended, cared for and celebrated until its natural end."[12] Indeed, they insist that their hospitality must be open to "gratuitous encounters" with the elderly, especially those who are most ill, "during which we are given the opportunity to listen to their life stories, their joys and difficulties, sometimes to share about the realities of faith and even to experience a time of prayer."

At times, these spiritual encounters — especially in the context of sickness (which, the Little Sisters are keen to note, can bring with it a special closeness to Christ) — change the residents and, at times, even the residents' family members. Sister Constance brings this up explicitly as one of the great gifts of the Little Sisters' ministry.[13] Indeed, the communal nature of their vocation — and their own care for their spiritual life — puts the Little Listers in a position to do this kind of work. The sisters cultivate a life of charity by committing to regular spiritual practices, as they share on their website:

- Daily Mass with our Sisters and the elderly
- Liturgy of the Hours sung in community (morning, evening and night prayer)
- Daily meditation, made together each morning
- A half-hour visit to the Blessed Sacrament each day
- Daily recitation of the rosary
- *Lectio Divina* and spiritual reading
- Sacrament of Reconciliation on a regular basis
- Habits of silence which help us cultivate intimacy with God. Our meals are usually taken in silence.
- We also enjoy several moments of retreat through-

out the year to refresh ourselves at the fountain of God's love.[14]

A counterculture of encounter and hospitality is made possible by the Little Sisters, who are spiritually healthy themselves — who have died to the world and are working together in community to offer older adults the kind of community in which they can live happy, flourishing lives. Indeed, Sister Constance is keen to point out a fact that may be surprising: Those who are entering their final phase of life, if provided for in the right way, are actually leading more flourishing lives than younger folks. She notes that "most of those age 80 and older say they're living their 'best possible life' or close to it, compared with one in five younger adults. ... Psychologically, people notice and prioritize the positive and let the negative go as they age."[15]

What a beautiful realization, especially given the fears that this book is trying to address. If (and this is a big if) we can give older adults a context in which their needs are met, then their lives can be more than just not bad; on the contrary, the final chapter of their lives, even in the face of very significant challenges, can be absolutely wonderful.

Calvary Hospice Hospital

Some reading this may think of hospice as a godsend, and that is indeed the experience of many people. But for others, the experience is something quite different. Indeed, private equity has purchased many hospice centers as a means of making a profit — with results that are predictably poor, terrible, and even deeply disturbing.[16] *Scientific American* notes that agencies have bribed doctors to bring them new patients, enrolled patients without their knowledge, and ditched patients when they approached the Medicare reimbursement limit. Some have gone to jail for fraud and other kinds of corruption.

Black Americans, in particular, are deeply distrustful of hospice care.[17] This comes, in part, as we saw earlier in this book, from a general distrust of a health-care system that has wronged their communities in so many ways over the centuries, ways that are still in this community's memories. But it comes also from a specific distrust of end-of-life practices. Too many hospices, motivated by and working within a consumerist throwaway culture, see these as populations that can be used to make money and then discarded when they are no longer profitable.

It is not at all surprising that Catholic nuns run wonderful hospice centers that resist these trends.[18] But in this third and final example in this chapter, we will focus on the project of a truly groundbreaking layman: Dr. Michael Brescia.[19] This pioneer in kidney dialysis took on the British tradition and basically cofounded the hospice tradition in the United States. After joining the House of Calvary in the Bronx in 1962, Dr. Brescia would transform the institution into Calvary Hospice Hospital — a world leader in palliative care at the end of life.

In an interview with the Sisters of Life, Dr. Brescia related the story of how he, a devout pro-life Catholic, was called to this work.[20] Unsurprisingly, he said, "God sent me," and it was his relationship with nuns that kickstarted his new mission:

> A couple of my colleagues asked me, "Michael, could you help us out? There are some nuns in the South Bronx that need a doctor to visit their patients tomorrow." So I said, "Ok, I'll do you a favor." The nuns gave me tea and cookies. At the end of the day, they said, "Oh, Dr. Brescia you were so helpful to our patients. Could you come back tomorrow?" I was on my way to the University of Pennsylvania to start a dialysis-transplant program. But I agreed to come back for just one more day.

When asked why he ended up staying, he said:

> The nuns also took in children that no one wanted, and they put the kids up to hanging on my legs as I was leaving so I would come back the next day. I loved the kids. The Sisters would say, "Stay another month." It got longer and longer. Unfortunately, the place was still going to close because there was not enough money. Calvary wasn't classified as a hospital yet, so I said, "Let's see if we can get approved." So the Joint Commission comes in and a Dr. Kruger looks at the place and says, "You're never going to pass. You've got too many serious deficiencies." But as I was showing him around he says, "Dr. Brescia, you've got a very famous name in kidneys. Do you know him?" I said, "I do ... I'm him!" He said, "Don't lie! You're not him. He's in Pennsylvania!" I said, "No, he's supposed to be in Pennsylvania, but he's right here in the South Bronx." At the end of it, Dr. Kruger says, "You've got six months to get these things fixed," but in the interim we went from getting $12 a day per patient to $300 and Calvary was saved. God kept me here, and He sent Dr. Kruger. The money came in, and we were able to develop. Then Cardinal Cooke came and said, "If you stay, if you set your mind to it, I have five acres in the North Bronx that I'll give to you to build a new Calvary."

Dr. Brescia described what came next as "torture." His family was packing to go to Pennsylvania as part of the relocation for his new and prestigious position running his dialysis-transplant program. He would end up staying in the Bronx by putting "my eyes on heaven instead of earth." Calvary became the only hospital of its kind in the world.

Calvary provides patients with wonderful care without even

a hint of aiming at or hastening the death of any of their patients. Here's their tagline: "We love you enough to never kill." When they come to a very difficult situation, they treat the symptoms until there is relief. "I'm never going to tell someone they have to suffer," Dr. Brescia has said. "I will work to alleviate their pain." And he makes the bold claim that absolutely any pain and any symptom can be alleviated. "There has never been a time when I said, 'I've got to go home and leave this person suffering because I don't know what to do.' I couldn't go home. I'd have to stay until I got rid of the pain. You can't allow someone to [lie] there in agony."

In part because Calvary refuses to leave people in agony, though they treat more than six thousand patients each year, "no one, after they have been here for 24 hours, asks for assisted suicide." It isn't that Calvary hasn't had terrible cases. But Brescia says that when you reach out with arms of love, when you treat the patient's room as a sanctuary, God's love is there too, and the patient can feel it. "When someone is dying, [do] you think that room is part of this earth?" asked Dr. Brescia. "No! You are not in this world. You have entered the vestibule of heaven."

In his answer to a question about the reasons people request physician-assisted killing, Dr. Brescia reflects much of what we have learned in this book already:

> It is because of suffering, depression, loneliness, physical symptoms, and personal image distortion. Sometimes people begin to feel guilty. They think, "Why should other people have to take care of me? Isn't it better if I'm dead?" That's the way the thinking starts. It is a hard thing when we have to depend on others to do very basic things for us. ... But the main way we suffer is emotionally — the sense of abandonment, the absence of love.

This, as we have seen, is primarily the result of a consumerist throwaway culture. Calvary responds with a counterculture of encounter and hospitality. "Emotional suffering," insists Brescia, "can only be treated by love." The first kind of love Calvary offers, as we have seen, is presence — just being there with the open arms of Christ. But the second part of loving is touch — holding and embracing.[21] Brescia says that you can't love without touch: "You must hold their hand! Hold them. They don't want pain medicine as much as they want touch, especially at the end. Take the nails out of their hands through touch." Finally, Calvary shows love to patients by speaking to them. All patients are told: "I love you; I will never desert you."

And the frame for everything they do? The Gospel, particularly the last mysteries of Christ's life. The suffering Christ motivates all that they do. The spiritual foundations of end-of-life care, according to Dr. Brescia, mirror Jesus' acknowledgment that he was giving all power and control over to his heavenly Father. When those at Calvary care for the dying, they understand that they are caring for Jesus — the suffering Christ.

• • •

We are now armed not only with the general ideas and values that show how a Catholic understanding of a good death can resist physician-assisted killing but also with the example of Christ, the saints, monks and friars, and contemporary people and institutions who have put these ideas and values into action in real life.

In the final section of this book, we will look at how to respond to the practical contemporary challenges facing Catholic individuals, families, communities, and institutions. The challenges, some of which I have already touched on, are substantial. But inspired by the boldness of examples provided by holy people such as Dr. Brescia, we can learn to keep our eyes on heaven and see what the Lord of both life and death may be calling us to.

CHAPTER SIX

Resisting Physician-Assisted Killing as Individuals

In some ways, it may seem odd to start this final section of the book with a focus on the individual. So much of what you have read about up to this point warns against individualism and isolation and emphasizes how human beings are made for (and flourish best when in) relationships with others. But even here, we will focus on how we as individuals have a relationship with ourselves and also with God. Indeed, a desire to die well — and therefore to live better — presumes a kind of relationship with both, doesn't it? We are self-aware, self-reflective, transcendent beings who can step outside ourselves, evaluate how we're doing relative to what God is asking of us, and work to change and improve. It is true that, in many contexts, this goes better when we have a family or other community, or both, checking in on us and helping us — and we will certainly examine these matters quite intentionally in the final two chapters of this book. But in this chapter, we will focus on what we can do as individuals to resist physician-assisted killing by living and dying well.

Living Well Morally

Recall that the *Ars Moriendi* tries to teach a large number of individual Christians from all different walks of life how to avoid temptations to various vices. Vices such as pride, impatience, despair, and avarice can derail us from having a good death. One of the key practices for avoiding these vices — a practice emphasized by Sts. Teresa of Ávila and Robert Bellarmine — is that of *dying to self*. That is, dying to the self of a world that emphasizes individual autonomy, control, consumerism, productivity, and so forth.

In his book *To Die Well*, Stephen Doran invokes Bellarmine specifically in his chapter "Dying to the World" and tells the story of Mary Ann, someone who died well because she had lived well.[1] In the eyes of the world, Doran notes, it looked as if Mary Ann's approaching death would be anything but good. She was confined to a wheelchair, her cognitive function had degenerated considerably, and she spent much of the day sleeping. But despite all of this, Mary Ann "remained a spiritual treasure trove," having spent a lifetime of devotion to the Triune God.

Sure, her spiritual life was no longer the roaring flame it once was, but there were still glowing embers present — white-hot beneath the surface, in fact — and those who visited her were able to feel them quite clearly at this final stage of her life. This time in the vestibule of heaven (to borrow Dr. Brescia's phrase) was obviously a sacred time for Mary Ann and those around her. Doran describes this time of transition between full awareness and unresponsiveness as a time "not to be rushed" but rather "to savor." Those around Mary Ann could tell that the process she was going through was a good and holy one.

Isn't it interesting that these sacred stages that stand between heaven and earth can produce such holiness? Again, from the world's perspective, there is little or nothing good about this final stage of life. But stories like that of Mary Ann suggest otherwise. We see something similar in the experience of St. Teresa of Ávila. Though she did not ultimately die from it, recall that she had an illness that put her in a similar liminal place between life and death, between time and space. And it was there that she had a transcendent experience. Her ego was changed, and she became a new kind of creature — one who would go on to become one of the most beloved saints of all time.

Like Saint Teresa, Mary Ann had been radically transformed by God's grace, and as Doran demonstrates, she died well in part because she had lived so well. Never attached to material things, she and her husband raised seven children on the wages of a telephone repairman. They never lacked for basic necessities, but they successfully resisted the consumerist throwaway culture. Indeed, it was in that detachment from the world that Mary Ann achieved a kind of contentment and peace; this stands in stark contrast to the anxiety-ridden lives of so many today. She was able to focus on the things that matter: the final things, the ultimate things.

By the end, Doran says, Mary Ann was stripped even further of her possessions. Everything the world values was basically gone, and she died very well indeed. Here is Doran's description of her very final moments:

> Periods of smiling wakefulness were increasingly replaced by sleep. Judicious doses of morphine helped ease her pain but precipitated even more somnolence. Once she was no longer able to eat or drink, death was imminent. Small groups of family huddled at her bed-

side, whispering decade after decade of the Rosary. With family beside her, she breathed her last literally seconds after the final decade of the Glorious Mysteries was recited. A good death indeed.

Mary Ann had lived out the truth that Saint Teresa reminds us of: that we have only one soul, only one death to die, only one life — and that there is only one Glory, which is eternal. As a result, there were many things for which Mary Ann did not care. She also lived according to Saint Francis's admonition: We must live as if the day of death is approaching and not let the world's cares and preoccupations turn us away from God and his commandments. Like Saint Joseph, Mary Ann had put aside the selfish will that the world wants to exploit with appeals to high status, pomp, and self-promotion. She was then free to subordinate herself to the will of God.

Even at the very end, when Mary Ann had nothing and was about to pass on, she was able to let her joy and gratitude radiate through her smiles. Again, according to the logic of the world, such joy and gratitude seem puzzling, if not absurd. But it turns out the foundational value that suggests that someone will have a good and even joyful death is *gratitude*. Fr. Mike Schmitz has found this in his experience of accompanying people who are dying.[2] He notes that he has seen even fifteen-year-olds die well if they have a sense of gratitude for the time they have been given, for the love and grace of God, and for the support and love of family and friends.

The key, again, is to die to our consumerist, individualist throwaway culture, which tells us that we are owed something — that what we have is "ours" in some way. Those who have this attitude and are faced with a situation in which they are forced to hand it back can be tempted to give in to fear and resentment. Father Mike notes that he has seen a dying man refuse to look at his newborn great-grandson because that little person has his whole life ahead of him while the man's was all behind him. But those who believe that everything about our lives is a gift, and that we are owed nothing, are able to die well because they are thankful for however many years they have been given. They recognize that their entire lives are not their own. Nothing belongs to us. Not one of the days we have on this earth is actually ours. As we learn from the perspective of Job: The Lord giveth, the Lord taketh away; blessed be the name of the Lord! (see 1:21). The Lord is the Giver of the gift of our lives, and it is a gift we in no way deserve.

In discussing the kind of prayers that should be prayed throughout the dying process, Allen Verhey insists on prayers of thanksgiving as an essential focus.[3] In a story he tells about a dying friend who is giving such thanks, it is clear that these prayers can be as simple as taking time to mention both small and great gifts that one has received from God: thanks for time at the end of life for a difficult relationship to be reconciled; thanks for pain relief to do final tasks and participate in events with family and friends; thanks for people in one's life who have enriched it — both through their support and through their challenges.

Significantly, Verhey's friend realizes through such prayer that, because there are so many gifts, "I wish I had started long ago. I wish there were more time for the task of gratitude."[4] This is an important insight for those who want to live well morally, in part as a means of dying well. Practicing gratitude, though good at the end of life, should be developed throughout our lives, well before we are faced with dying. Seeing everything we have in life as a gift from God is a lens we should cultivate *now*. Thanking people in our lives for what they have done for us should be happening *now*. Holding on less tightly to the gifts we have been given, as if we are owed them, should begin *now*. And prayers of thanksgiving to God should be on our minds, hearts, and lips *now*.

Happily, there are many spiritual practices available to help us with this stuff — especially with that last part.

Living Well Spiritually

Few of us will serve others in the face of death and dying the way the Little Sisters of the Poor do. They have accepted a vocation to face these challenges, but we should nevertheless take a cue from the attention they give to care for their own spiritual lives. We should look at the examples from the previous chapter afresh — this time, for ourselves: daily Mass, Liturgy of the Hours (morning, evening, and night), daily meditation, a half-hour visit to the Blessed Sacrament each day, daily recitation of the Rosary, *lectio divina* and spiritual reading, the Sacrament of Reconciliation on a regular basis, habits of silence, and several moments of retreat throughout the year.

That's a lot. And, again, few of us are called to do all of this at this level of frequency. But surely each of us can find something significant on this list that we can and should incorporate more intentionally into our lives in order to care for our spiritual health and our relationship with God. So many opportunities are here, for instance, to incorporate Bellarmine's insistence that we should be making frequent space in our lives to examine our consciences on our way toward dying to the world. There are also many opportunities for keeping our future deaths close and present to our minds and hearts, including when we pray, as the Lord himself asked us, to be spared the final test.

Recall also that keeping our future deaths close and present to our minds and hearts honors Jesus' warning that we know neither the day nor the hour when death is coming for us, and we therefore need to be hyperaware that this moment could come at any time. We need to avoid the behavior of the fool, who, putting death out of his mind, builds huge barns for himself to store up all his goods. Recall Michael Connelly's reminder that the practice of keeping our future death close and present to our minds and hearts helps us resist the many temptations that can cause us to lose focus on what our lives are ultimately about.

Earlier in this book, I briefly mentioned the Christian tradition of memento mori, an ancient practice that, happily, has received renewed interest in our time. Perhaps no person is more responsible for that renewed interest in remembering our death than Sr. Theresa Aletheia Noble.[5] A former atheist, she was prompted to start exploring questions of the afterlife with more seriousness after the death of her friend. That process eventually led her first to theism and then to Catholicism.

In part because her journey to the Faith began with a meditation on death, Sr. Theresa Aletheia made memento mori a central part of her ministry — even writing a book on the topic.[6] In particular, she wrote it as an "Advent companion" after learning that it used to be common during Advent for pastors to preach on the Four Last Things: death, judgment, hell, and heaven. She lamented the fact that too many of our post-Christian holiday celebrations are filled with self-centered sentimentality, which keeps us from focusing on matters of ultimate concern.

Sister Theresa's book has regular prayers and reflections, but she also created, for those who want a reminder each day, a memento mori calendar with quotes from Scripture, Church Fathers, saints, and other contemporary thinkers about the importance of remembering our death.[7] Other recommended practices include displaying the ancient symbol of a skull on one's desk or in another prominent place where it can remind us that we are dust and to dust we shall return. In addition, we can make a practice of visiting and caring for the graves of others — and praying for those specific dead — especially if it appears that few are around to pray for them.

And speaking of graves, part of what it means to keep one's death in mind involves preparing for events surrounding the dying process. Here are some things to bear in mind in this regard: Do you have a clear relationship with a priest who can offer you anointing of the sick? Do loved ones in your life know about your preferences for advanced directives, your wake, your funeral, and your burial preferences? And remember the *Ars Moriendi*'s suggestion that you have a partner to help shepherd you through the dying process? Make sure to have a plan for this too. Check out the appendix of this book for resources related to these important considerations.

Of course, all of this requires resisting a culture that pushes us toward individualism and isolation, in which this kind of communication becomes difficult, if not impossible.

Against Individualism

Several times now, we've confronted the terrible fact that more and more people are dying alone. Avoiding an isolated death is one of the reasons physician-assisted killing can seem like a less-bad option for so many people. But as Marianna Orlandi has argued, a big part of resisting a culture of individualism, which leads to these kinds of deaths, is choosing not to live alone — that is, choosing not to live solely for oneself.[8]

What this means is that we need to make a conscious effort to live life, Orlandi says, as "a relational, communal, sacrificial, and generative experience." This presents what is, in some ways, a classically Catholic and even Trinitarian paradox about relationship: We, as individuals, need to choose consciously not to lead lives that idolatrously focus on ourselves, especially when we make an idol of our secular myths of individual autonomy and independence. Here's how Orlandi puts it:

> Lonely deaths are the inevitable product of our *independent* lives, the necessary outcome of decades spent "focusing on ourselves" as our culture mandates. They are

the natural consequence of hours dedicated to running on a treadmill instead of chasing children; of hundreds of hours studying privately, uninterrupted by conversations with friends and peers who might have slowed us down; of hectic sleep schedules that prevent us from taking part in our friends' plans and parties; of choosing solitary meals over shared ones. Such a focus on oneself is typical of today's culture across the board.

And she notes that this is not at all a problem merely for single people who aren't living in nuclear families. Married people still leave their elderly parents alone in care homes — and some support (or even encourage) PAK. Married people with families can and often do make an idol of their education and career paths. Caregiving can still be seen as something beneath them that should be outsourced to someone else (or, in the case of a caregiving robot, to some*thing* else). Too often, the forces that form us, says Orlandi, are about demanding what we are owed rather than learning how to offer self-gift to the other. In many cases, unfortunately, this is not a natural instinct. Effective resistance to U.S.-style individualism often must be cultivated and learned.

Orlandi also encourages us to remember our finitude. It is through this kind of remembrance, she argues, that "we won't only *see* our ailing parents, relatives, and friends. We will also recognize how much at every stage of life *we are them:* in dire need of attention, care, and love." We need to focus on our neediness and finitude now. The idolatry-enabling illusions provided by smartphones, social media, and (increasingly) AI "companions," Orlandi adds, are merely "filling our hollow hearts with things that — as my mom wisely says — won't bring us tea when we are old and sick."

Of course, if we want to be the ones bringing tea to our old and sick parents, we will need to be physically present to actually bring them tea. This means making choices — often before one may choose to get married and raise a family — to remain physically close to one's parents. Getting a particular job and pursuing a career is not unimportant, but being around to aid one's parents as they age, decline, and die is likely more important. The duty to honor our parents is one of the most important unchosen obligations we have. And the fulfillment of this duty will often require resisting the temptation to simply abandon one's family in full pursuit of a career. This may not be possible for many families who have already, for many reasons, made choices to live far apart from one another — but that means we must be vigilant and ready to make sacrifices for the sake of being close to parents or other family members when they are elderly and in need of assistance.

And let's be honest about something here: Sometimes the temptation to pursue a career instead of staying near family comes from one's parents! Instead of being part of the resistance to a culture of individualism and autonomy, parents are often the ones encouraging children to go out, spread their wings, and fend for themselves quite apart from their families. And though there will be times when this makes sense, parents should resist the current cultural expectation that this is simply the default option for children. Instead, the default option (which, again, of course, admits exceptions) should be that children will be around to get their parents tea when they are old and sick.

A few years ago, Gilbert Meilaender wrote a classic article, titled "I Want to Burden My Loved Ones," that makes precisely this case.[9] A veteran of debates about assisted suicide and so many other bioethical topics, Meilaender, in making his provocative case, first turns to his own lived experience: He has sweated in the hot sun playing ball, played kiddie games he detests, sat through mind-numbing recitals and concerts, exhausted himself running beside little bicycles, waited for untold hours in clothing stores — and so much more — all for his children. Isn't it time for his children to be burdened by him? Believe it or not, this argument is not without merit.

But it is so much more than that. Meilaender acknowledges that while care for his children produced real burdens, those experiences were at the same time — "almost miraculously" — *also sources of great joy and meaning.* The significance of a family is deeply connected to these kinds of unchosen obligations, which bind us together in love. But this is where Meilaender, when he hears parents speak of not wanting to burden their children as they age and reach the final stages of their lives, gets so annoyed. Haven't these parents taught their children that they will experience a similar, almost miraculous situation in which they will experience real burdens caring for their parents but also feel similarly privileged and joyful about the opportunity to do so?

Recall that the fear of becoming a burden drives a lot of people to choose or support PAK. In order to resist PAK, then, those of us who are parents, rather than trying to shield our children from burdens, should instead help them understand burdens in the proper context and with a proper attitude. And we do that primarily by teaching them through our example: by making it clear that it is our privilege and a joy to help them bear their burdens. But we also teach this lesson by putting our own pride aside and showing them that we are happy to have them bear our burdens as well.

Encounter and Hospitality > Consumerism and Throwaway Culture

In any given human story, especially in the midst of our consumerist throwaway culture, there may, of course, be multiple reasons why one would be tempted to live out a life of individualism and isolation — a life in which one's own death and the deaths of one's loved ones is simply not a concern. But, as we've already seen, many of these cases are produced by a common set of concerns: consumerism and prestige. The culture teaches us that one simply must have a certain salary and standard of living in order to flourish. This includes a certain house size and car performance, an acceptable wardrobe and standard of vacations, and a career trajectory that contains a certain level of status.

Of course, holy figure after holy figure — including the Son of God, the Second Person of the Trinity himself — has warned us about the poison of these kinds of temptations. These temptations not only fool us into thinking that we are autonomous beings in charge of our lives. They not only disconnect and displace us from our families by pushing us to follow the money and the job wherever they take us. They not only keep us from understanding the burden of serving others as a joyful privilege and even from learning how to genuinely care for another person in the first place. They not only risk trapping us in assumptions that turn people into the most aggressive supporters and users of PAK. More than all of this, these kinds of temptations threaten our very salvation.

We've seen Jesus make this absolutely clear. We've seen the countercultural example of the humble Saint Joseph. We've seen how Saints Francis and Teresa also made this a central message of their lives and work. We've seen St. Robert Bellarmine insist that "the deceitful error of the rich" risks keeping us from being saved and from dying a good death — unless we diligently "enquire, either by our own reading and meditation, or by consulting holy and learned men, whether our 'superfluous' riches can be retained without sin, or whether we ought of necessity to give them to the poor."

This is very often not easy, especially because of the power that our consumerist throwaway culture has over most of us. Even the very holy Dr. Brescia described as "torture" the choice put before him: continuing to pursue the prestigious job that took him away from serving his local Bronx area or staying home and putting himself at the service of a population who bear the Holy Face of Christ as the least among us. This man put money and prestige aside, and the rest is history. No one lived out the counterculture of encounter and hospitality, welcoming the sick and dying into a real community of embodied love, better than Dr. Brescia.

To be sure, not all of us can devote our entire lives to this work, like the founder of Calvary Hospice Hospital or the Carmelite Sisters of Los Angeles or the Little Sisters of the Poor. But there is so much at stake — for resisting PAK, yes, and also (again) for our very salvation — that we simply must find a way to be part of the counterculture of encounter and hospitality. What follows are some suggestions for orienting our lives as individuals in these contexts.

If you are in a position to do so, consider a first or second career, or intense service projects (perhaps as part of your retirement), that will put you at the service of the elderly, the mentally ill (especially those with dementia), the disabled, and the terminally ill. Especially given the antinatalism in the developed West, coupled with our aging population, the number of people in need of this kind of care dwarfs the number of available family members and others capable of offering it. Sure, we could slouch toward fooling the elderly via robot "caregivers" — and this looks like where our culture is heading — but the human dignity of those who bear the Face of Christ means they are owed the loving words and touch of a real human being.

Does this seem like a lot to take on? Perhaps it would take you out of your current career, making it difficult for you to pay your mortgage or other bills. These are real problems, to be sure, but so many individuals today find themselves trapped in jobs they loathe because of such consumerist considerations. I urge you to take this intention to prayer. God may be calling you to step out in trust and to let go of the things you think provide security and, instead, to put yourself in a position to work toward building a culture of encounter and hospitality for these vulnerable populations — those who are Christ calling out to us.

If that isn't realistic right now, perhaps because of your commitments to family (we will discuss specific issues related to families in the next chapter), there are a host of other options open to you. Make time to regularly and formally volunteer in a nursing home, especially one that serves people with dementia and others at risk for PAK. Such service signals publicly the equal human dignity of these populations, and it can also mitigate the slide toward robot "care." Also consider taking the time to bring a colleague, neighbor, or friend who isn't as plugged into these issues to accompany you on your volunteer visits and encourage more encounters between younger and older generations. The power of such encounters is such that simply being in the space of those who bear the Face of Christ this way can be transformative. You never know what the results of these encounters may be, for the seeds, once planted, take on a life of their own.

You can also work to get government and other resources to empower families to take care of their elderly and disabled loved ones at home. This is an important goal on multiple levels, but it is also much more cost-effective than care in nursing homes.[10] There are so many reasons why it is better for loved ones to be cared for and allowed to die at home. But for those whose care, for one reason or another, needs to be in a clinical or care-home context, we can also work to get government and other resources to provide significantly better care in nursing homes and other care institutions, including better pay for employees and reimbursement rates from insurance companies. This is a wonderful way for Catholics to serve as bridge figures in our hyperpolarized and idolatrous political environment. Pro-lifers who identify with the Right have overlapping consensus with social-justice activists who identify with the Left on these issues — in ways that beg for us all to unite in this common cause.

Finally, do all of this in a very public way. Let your light shine before all by putting it on a lampstand and not under a bushel basket (see Mt 5:15). Our consumerist throwaway culture finds ways to discard our vulnerable populations quietly, away from the public eye, without public discussion or scrutiny. So we need to make as many people as possible aware of these vulnerable populations and their need for protection. Post about your service regularly on social media. Discuss it with the people you encounter. Normalize the idea of orienting one's life in service to the populations facing these challenges. Tell stories about how your work in this area has transformed your life. Declaring to the world that it is a privilege and a joy to encounter and care for these populations is an essential part of what it means to resist our throwaway culture and proclaim the Gospel in our time.

CHAPTER SEVEN

Resisting Physician-Assisted Killing as Families

Much of what we discussed in the previous chapter on resisting physician-assisted killing as individuals transfers directly to thinking about how the family can resist PAK. We will focus immediately below on bringing death into the home. As we read in the last chapter, Mary Ann experienced a good death in large part because her family was able to gather around her, pray with her, and support her as she passed. Bringing death into the home also helps everyone in the home to live out memento mori because death — real death — is no longer something "out there" to be ignored or kept out of polite circles. Those who are dying will often express to family members what their preferences are with regard to final things, such as wakes, funerals, and burials. And in healthy families, isolated individualism cannot survive.

As both Marianna Orlandi and Gilbert Meilaender make clear, the practice of being a family habituates the individual to think first not of himself but of the unplanned and unchosen obligations one has to another.

These others can then become serious partners in expanding that care and concern. Perhaps one person brings a family member along to volunteer in a nursing home. Perhaps whole families take on service projects focused on care for the elderly, the mentally ill (especially those with dementia), the disabled, and the terminally ill. Some families may even start their own care homes or other institutions (perhaps in partnership with the local church — see more on this in the final chapter) aimed at serving and caring for these populations. When families do these kinds of things together, it becomes even easier to share the light of the Gospel before all — allowing it to shine on populations that so many would prefer to keep marginalized, out of sight, and out of mind.

Regular prayer and other spiritual practices are also more impactful in the context of a family. As we've seen in both the historical and contemporary religious communities engaged thus far, the social expectation that one needs to show up for prayer is a powerful one. It is not just an individual commitment, not just a commitment to God, but also a commitment to the community with whom one lives in intimate quarters. You go to Mass together. You pray before meals together. You go to adoration together. You say evening prayer together. You pray the Rosary together. You call each other out for not going to confession regularly enough. You take time to enjoy God's creation together by going on walks, hikes, bike rides, and the like. You even take family retreats once or twice a year for spiritual renewal.

In the first half of this chapter we will, as just mentioned, focus on what it means to bring death into the home and to resist an individualist, consumerist throwaway culture. In the second half, we will focus on two stories of families that illustrate much of what we are talking about, to help individuals and families imagine what this may look like in real life — including in challenging situations in which families are not set up to live out the vision perfectly.

Bringing Death into the Home

We are faced with a paradox with regard to death in our culture. On the one hand, you might think that — what with video games, films, and true crime stories — there is already enough death being brought into your home. You may even have good reason to think there is *too much* death being brought into your home.

But this kind of death, of course, is anything but real. The blood exploding across the screen and the limbs flying apart are sometimes literally cartoonish props. The recent film *Deadpool and Wolverine* played the pop song "Bye Bye Bye" by NSYNC in the background while this violence and killing was happening — interspersed with the title character doing a dance from the quarter-century-old music video. Far from engaging death in a serious way, this kind of death is mediated into our lives in a way that is fundamentally and intentionally unreal and unserious.

How do we know? Because when real dying and death come for our family members, well, most of us push it about as far away as we possibly can. So uncomfortable are we with death that we will discard the sick and the dying in either highly medicalized and technologized clinical contexts or into hopelessly understaffed and desperately lonely nursing homes, which essentially serve as way stations toward death, where residents spend their final days mindlessly watching TV or staring off into space (or, as we've seen folks move in the other direction, trying to take control of death through physician-assisted killing). We already noted how, only two generations ago, the bodies of those who had died at home used to be regularly and prominently displayed in people's homes for visitation and viewing. But today we almost never see dead bodies outside of funeral homes, and even that is becoming less and less common. Indeed, one significant reason people support PAK is precisely the fear of being present with death and those nearing it.[1]

We need a counterculture of encounter and hospitality that will bring the sick, the dying, and the dead back into the home, both literally and figuratively — figuratively in the sense that we need to talk about death and dying as families and even with fairly young children. Death in general — and also the coming death of family members — should not be a taboo subject. The death of a grandparent or another family member should not be the first time the subject comes up. Indeed, regular daily occurrences, such as driving by a cemetery, provide the chance to talk in age-appropriate ways about the topic. And from there you might visit a cemetery, perhaps to visit the graves of family members and friends, and maybe even, as suggested previously, to pray for the forgotten dead. You might consider tending to unkept graves and putting flowers or other mementos by them.

Telling our children about the lives of friends and family who have passed away could lead to stories about how they died and even discussion of the good and bad things about their deaths. And this could eventually lead to discussions about one's own death and preparing for it in all sorts of good and healthy ways. This also helps children, from a young age, to come to a healthy understanding of what it means to have death inform one's life — first by seeing a parent live this way and then letting it bubble up in their own minds and hearts. It may help to invoke the examples of Saint Joseph and of Jesus — and of Jesus' having to face the death of his beloved earthly father and what that must have been like for both of them.

But we should literally bring death back into the home as

well. Especially when, again, the alternatives seem to be highly medicalized or lonely care-home contexts, it should come as no surprise that about eight in ten people in the United States prefer to die at home. Recall L.S. Dugdale's moving account of why that might be:

> There remains a certain constancy to home life — pets and people, to be sure, but also *that* chair, *that* painting, *that* perennial plant. The home is where we feast and celebrate, weep and mourn, sit and stare. ... Home accepts us at our most authentic. Home embraces us, silently consoling us with the knowledge that we belong to *this* home. Why would we die anywhere else?[2]

This option doesn't make as much money for clinical health-care providers, and it may not maximize the hours or days someone has to live, but for those who are near the end of life, it may be the most dignified, relational, and holy way to live out their remaining time on this earth. Plus, it provides an unavoidable lesson in memento mori, both for the family members and for visitors, that can help reconnect those around the dying person in a real, authentic way to what it means to die well. It also avoids the twin idolatrous temptations (wrought of the harmful illusions of autonomy and control) that involve fighting for extended life at any cost or taking death into one's own hands. Dying at home allows for the powerful public witness of resisting death when appropriate and also discerning the time to accept and even welcome death gracefully as a gift from God — again, as part of a choice about how to live, not a choice to die.

It would be the height of unrealism to suggest that this kind of choice is an easy one. It is not — especially if, as we will see below and in the next chapter, there just aren't enough resources (or time) available to care for one's family member properly at home. Recall the story of the death of Brother Vincent in chapter 5: Even in the midst of a large, wonderful community with plenty of resources, his death took a terrible toll on his religious family. But when we make time for praying together, touching together, remembering together, forgiving together, and simply being quiet together, grace-filled and mysterious things happen. Deaths can be transformed by God's grace and experienced as joyful events. The family is taught that sick and dying family members aren't just old people taking up space but are fully human and dignified individuals who bear the Holy Face of Christ in a special way. And, like the brothers who cared for their brother Vincent, the caregivers are themselves transformed by the process. In the case of Brother Vincent, fragile and nervous brothers became rocks. And they did that and became that together: as family.

Resisting the Traps of Isolated Consumer Culture

Consumer-style isolation can look different in a family than it does with individuals, but it comes from similar places and concerns that we've already addressed: consumerism and prestige. Families can also absorb the cultural lie that one simply must have a certain salary and standard of living; own a certain kind of house, wardrobe, and car; enjoy luxurious vacations; and remain on a career trajectory that contains a certain kind of status. But also, quite apart from any choices one makes along these lines, families who want to live in even modest houses that fit their size can also be — through no fault of their own — caught in what is sometimes called the "two-income trap." That is, both the mom and the dad in a family feel that they simply must work in order to pay the mortgage on their home and pay for their car, gas, groceries, children's activities, and so on.

Here, Catholic social teaching plays a significant role in how we might think about these matters. Not enough attention has been paid to the social and economic structures that have led to the consumerist mindset and the two-income trap. In particular, we need to pay attention not only to how this affects the elderly and their care but also to how it affects children and parental care for children. Let's look at this important passage from Pope St. John Paul II's *Laborem Excercens*. It is worth meditating on and absorbing what is being said here about social structures and how they affect family life:

> It should also be noted that the justice of a socioeconomic system and, in each case, its just functioning, deserve in the final analysis to be evaluated by the way in which man's work is properly remunerated in the system. ... A just wage is the concrete means of *verifying the justice* of the whole socioeconomic system and, in any case, of checking that it is functioning justly. It is not the only means of checking, but it is a particularly important one and, in a sense, the key means. This means of checking concerns above all the family. Just remuneration for the work of an adult who is responsible for a family means remuneration which will suffice for establishing and properly maintaining a family and for providing security for its future. Such remuneration can be given either through what is called a *family wage* — that is, a single salary given to the head of the family for his work, sufficient for the needs of the family without the other spouse having to take up gainful employment outside the home — or through *other social measures* such as family allowances or grants to mothers devoting themselves exclusively to their families. These grants should correspond to the actual needs, that is, to the number of dependents for as long as they are not in a position to assume proper responsibility for their own lives. ...

> It will redound to the credit of society to make it possible for a **mother** — without inhibiting her freedom, without psychological or practical discrimination, and without penalizing her as compared with other women — to devote herself to taking care of her **children and educating them in accordance with their needs, which vary with age**. Having to abandon these tasks in order to take up paid work outside the home is wrong from the point of view of the good of society and of the family when it contradicts or hinders these primary goals of the mission of a **mother**.
>
> In this context it should be emphasized that, on a more general level, the whole labor process must be organized and adapted in such a way as to respect the requirements of the person and his or her forms of life, above all life in the home, taking into account the individual's age and sex.[3]

Again, the passage above is a discussion about caring for children and thus focuses on the unique role of mothers in doing that. But what if we changed the bolded words above to refocus the message on caring for one's elders — and, in particular, aging parents and grandparents? The same basic message would and should apply, especially if we reject the isolation of the nuclear family and expand the notion to include a more traditional understanding of who counts as family. Indeed, the Pontifical Academy for Life has insisted that honoring our elderly means that "every effort must be made to enable the elderly to live in a 'family' environment during this phase of life."[4]

What does this mean, practically speaking?

Let's talk first about those who have the financial and other resources to make choices along these lines. First, we should take special care to reject the idea — one that is in some ways new and peculiar to our own time and place — that "family" just means the nuclear family, apart from grandparents, aunts, uncles, and cousins. When possible, we should focus on living together in thick, extended familial communities in which we are physically around to help each other — and, in particular, to help our aging parents.

As already discussed, we should resist the temptation to live far away from family members who would support us, or to live far from those whom we have a familial obligation to support. Indeed, in a Catholic context, it makes sense that "Who is going to look after our parents?" should be a question asked as part of the pre-Cana process before a couple gets married. Of course, the answer to that question gets even more complicated if Mom and Dad live in different places: Divorce is damaging for so many reasons (including to children), but it rears its ugly head in this context as well, as it very often pulls the connections and supports of families apart when they are needed most.

It is one thing to talk about the great good of an extended familial community, but it is quite another for *there to actually be an extended family around*. In so many places in the consumerist West, we are seeing social and economic pressures leading to ever-lower birthrates. This means that, in many cases, there simply won't be family around! We should therefore refuse to artificially limit the number of children we bear, adopt, or foster.

Again, there are issues related to economic privilege: Not everyone will be able to, but those who can should make choices about housing, debt, and living situations that allow them to care for a wide range of family members, especially parents and other older relatives. So many otherwise privileged people get caught in the drive of consumerism, which causes them to become "house poor" or "debt poor" — especially in ways that force families into the kind of two-income trap that handcuffs them to jobs or places, or both, and keeps them from attending to the needs of older family members. Attending to such needs could mean going to visit them and care for them in their homes or apartments, but it may very well mean welcoming older family members into one's own home when the time calls for it. Ultimately, we need to make sure our loved ones are cared for and loved by people who love them — not by machines or by overworked and underpaid staff who put them in chemical straitjackets because there are so few resources available for their care.

We will discuss this in more detail in the next chapter, but let's be clear once again that not all families have the economic and other privileges necessary to live out this vision. And that means that individuals, families, and especially larger communities and institutions need to work hard to get economic and other resources to families so they can. But, for now, let's turn to two real-life stories that illustrate much of what we have been discussing.

They Didn't Always Have Newark

John Soriano, writing his family's story in *First Things*, captures much of what this chapter is extolling and also what it is warning about.[5] Indeed, in many ways, the change in John's family signals much about how we got into this mess and what we need to do to combat the problem. Recall our discussion of how many immigrants from different social contexts find what we do to our elderly, disabled, and dying relatives in the secularized West to be unthinkable. Well, John begins his story by describing his traditional family living in Newark, New Jersey, a family that was much closer in culture and spirit to the immigrant Italian culture of the late nineteenth century than it was to the 2022 U.S. culture in which he was writing his piece.

He begins with the aftermath of his parents' wedding in 1953. Did they move into a new home or even their own apartment? No, they moved onto one floor of a Newark three-family house owned by his grandparents. His aunt lived on the first floor, and his grandparents squeezed into the middle one, and this way of life lasted for several years and saw the birth of multiple children. Here are some other great details from his story. Notice the beautiful simplicity of life together there:

> The three homes were tied together not only by a grand oak front staircase, but also by a rickety backstairs, where everything important happened (usually at a hundred decibels). You always had a babysitter and a good meal on call. Life was frugal, by today's standards, but good. The whole edifice smelled perpetually of competing "gravies" — Newarkese for "sauce" — from the three kitchens.

John was keen to emphasize how, in the mid-1970s, his grandpa, when he got sick and started to decline, was cared for in this home. "There was always someone around to help him bathe, use the bathroom, and so on," we are told. "He wasn't in good shape — but he was never lonely."

Fast-forward to the late nineties, after the death of John's father, and the situation was much different. His mother was left alone in quite a different place: the suburban ranch home to which she and her husband had moved. She had good friends and good neighbors (which not everyone can say), but "she was lonely and bereft." All four of her children lived so far away that "daily visits [were] implausible given our work and family obligations." John had young kids, which also made traveling difficult. But he would do his best to ride the bus from his New York law-firm job to his mother's house to spend the night during the months following his dad's passing. Needless to say: "It was a tough time."

His mom then remarried (a friend named Charlie), and after several good years in their home together, they sold it and moved into a senior living facility, which John describes as very nice. It was the kind of place where, if you pay a very heavy entrance fee, you could first live in a nice independent apartment, then move to assisted living, and then to nursing care, all on the same premises. When Charlie got sick, however, he went straight to nursing care. And what came next was also quite tough:

> The bad news was that, after Charlie passed, Mom was alone again. Surrounded by lovely friends, yes. But ultimately still alone.
>
> Several years after Charlie's passing, Mom's Parkinson's disease started to kick in. Despite good care, medicine, and physical therapy, Mom deteriorated steadily. She needed a walker, then a scooter. And then she couldn't really manage either of those. She needed us more than ever.
>
> We "kids" — the youngest of us is sixty — visit often. But we don't live around the corner, and we have the competing obligations of work, children, and grandchildren.

John's mom lived through the tough years of COVID but endured it all, including the thousands dying as a result of New Jersey's governor sending so many infected patients into nursing homes and other care facilities. The family continues to visit, but many of them notice how short-staffed even this nice facility is. At times, they discuss the possibility of moving their mother into one of their homes, but the details of their lives — including the raw difficulty of needing tremendous physical strength — get in the way. The care facility has a special lift for changing and bathing. John's final reflections are so poignant and relevant to what we are discussing here:

> So Mom remains at the nursing facility, where she is cared for well. When we visit, she often says, "I'm ready to go

home now," not realizing that she is "home now." That hurts, especially when we have to inevitably end our visit and she says, "Don't leave me. Please take me with you."

Knowing what we know now, I think it would have been better if Mom had moved in with one of us after Charlie died. The COVID-induced isolation — and worse — permeating our "senior living facilities" is a haunting reminder that, as a society, we lost something precious by migrating away from multi-generational living.

That three-family house in Newark is looking pretty good.

The lessons from this story speak for themselves — although perhaps it is good to remind ourselves that John's mother, despite the limitations John so powerfully describes, was one of the lucky ones.

Bringing Frank Home

Next, let's look at the story that Noreen Madden McInnes relays in her wonderful book *Keep at It, Riley: Accompanying My Father through Death into Life*. Noreen's story, in some ways, overlaps with the one John told. This time, we are engaging with a deeply Irish family that also brought family-centered practices with them from the old country. In thinking about rituals surrounding death in the time of her great-grandmother, for instance, Noreen writes the following:

> The Irish Vigil is known as "The Wake," which means to stay awake and watch over the body through the night until they are buried in the ground. ...
>
> In [my great-grandmother's] day, she and other women would come into the home of the deceased to wash the body and prepare it to be "laid-out" in the front

room of the house, known as the "parlor." That's why we still hear funeral homes referred to as "funeral parlors" today. Mom Conway would also have given your parlor an upgrade by borrowing better rugs, paintings, and furniture from around the neighborhood. Today she'd be called a home stager, making sure you were looking good for the party. Party? Well, absolutely. It's the Irish custom to honor their dead and to pay their respects to the family by showing up at the house with their hands full of food and whiskey.[6]

Like John, Noreen moved away from this tight-knit Irish family in Mountain Top, Pennsylvania, to build a family with her husband, Peter, in San Diego, California. But as her parents began to decline, the loss was felt more acutely — especially by her parents. One day, when Noreen called to tell them she was going to Africa on a missionary trip for two weeks, they responded by asking, poignantly, "Can we be your Africa?"

That led Noreen to visit her folks for two weeks; and it was clear they did not simply need her company — they needed her help. Her father, Frank, was already pretty sick with a number of issues and needed an extra large wheelchair to fit his large frame and get around. Her mother was slowing down and would get forgetful. One day during her visit, Noreen got the terrible news that her mother had been killed in car accident. Further weakened by the loss, and with no spouse to care for him, Frank needed to be placed in a local skilled-nursing facility. But one day Frank called Noreen and said, "Get me out of here. ... I feel like I'm in a concentration camp."[7] Noreen had him removed immediately and had him stay instead in a facility run by the local Carmelite Sisters, who — as readers of this book will not find surprising — gave him much better care. Noreen went home to her husband and children feeling good about things.

One day, however, she got a call from Frank's doctor and heard the news she had been dreading: Frank was dying, and she needed to move quickly to see him before the end. But, remarkably, upon seeing his daughter in person, Frank rallied! The very next day, in fact, he said he would go down to work on his rehab. All the nurses told Noreen that she needed to stay in Pennsylvania because her dad was doing so much better with her there in person. But what about her husband and children? She couldn't leave them in California. Noreen went to pray by her mother's grave and asked for help with her decision — and then suddenly the idea came to her: She would ask her father to move in with her in California.

Frank originally said no because he had always insisted that he didn't want to be a burden on his children, but Noreen fought back, and it became a battle of two stubborn Irish spirits. Eventually Frank relented and agreed to come. Then Noreen realized that, though they had talked about the idea from time to time, she hadn't cleared the idea with her husband, Peter. But he said yes immediately, and after a difficult trip in a medical RV, Noreen's family welcomed Frank into their home on Christmas.

This very sick, very large man (he was six and a half feet tall) who couldn't walk and whose wheelchair didn't fit through the guestroom doorframe, was now living in their dining room, with curtains in the doorways for privacy. Peter created custom ramps so Frank could use the back patio and other places in the house. He even created an outdoor shower for Frank to use (his double-wide wheelchair wouldn't fit through a traditional bathroom door), always with plenty of privacy, in the often-wonderful San Diego weather. Peter and Noreen regularly brought in a certified nursing assistant and a registered nurse to help with specialized tasks and medicines and other aspects of Frank's care.

The initial euphoria of having him home gave way to what were often different or banal realities of helping care for Frank: helping manage his twenty-plus medications, cooking the kinds of food he was interested in eating, managing all the letters and calls from people back home. But everyone helped out: kids, neighbors, and even the dogs. Noreen loved the new routine and loved having her father in her home, especially the mornings, with the coffee, newspaper, and Frank telling story after endless, wonderful, and often hilarious story. Late morning meant a walk in the neighborhood, where this big, gregarious man would charm all the neighbors. One time, the daughter of a neighbor sweetly asked her mother, "Mom, how come we like Frank so much?"

Frank always led grace before meals — even when he was too weak to get out of bed (they rolled his bed into the dining room in those situations). It was a wonderful time — until it wasn't. Frank's health got worse, and he required hospitalization. Noreen had discussions with him about aggressive measures and resuscitation. Frank basically wanted everything done: "Give me a chance," he told his daughter. And she did — until things got really bad with his health and he once again changed his mind. "I want to go home," Frank told his daughter. He knew that hospice, dying, and death awaited him there. But he wanted it all in the space his family had created for him. He died in his new home — which was also his daughter's home — and then his family brought his body back to Mountain Top to have an Irish wake where everyone could visit and pay their final respects.

After the funeral, the family had a final luncheon, as was their custom for such events in Mountain Top. Many toasts were offered. Noreen narrates her husband's toast this way:

> Peter paused for a long moment.
> "You know, many think that it was a hardship for us to care for Frank. I have to admit that I had my concerns about the plan. Frank was an invalid. He had an amazing number of health issues. He was traveling far from his beloved Mountain Top. It was going to be a huge disrup-

tion to our lives."

Another pause. Peter continued emotionally.

"Welcoming Frank into our home turned out to be one of the best things that ever happened to me. My children got the opportunity to spend time with their grandfather that they never had due to the distance. Noreen and Frank broadened and deepened their relationship. I had the chance to better know a man whose strength and good humor amazed me on a daily basis. It was one of the biggest blessings of my life." Peter raised his glass, "To Frank."

There wasn't a dry eye in the room.[8]

The six months of his living in San Diego had not only been wonderful for Frank; they had also been wonderful — life-changing — for those who cared for him. In an interview after she published her book, Noreen described the situation much as Peter did.[9] She described its falling to her to care for Frank "as a mistake," at least by the logic of the world. A choir director and liturgist, she had no significant medical knowledge, and she had always been squeamish around illness. She describes herself as perhaps the last person on the planet equipped to give Frank what he needed — and yet, with God's grace, she came through at the right time and was forever changed as a result. "My father blessed me more than I blessed him," she said.

Another story that speaks for itself.

As mentioned, the final chapter of this book will bring to bear much of what we saw in this chapter and the previous chapter together, inviting us to think about how to respond as larger communities and institutions. After all, both John and Noreen were in privileged positions and could bring significant resources to bear. Many more people will need the help of their broader communities in order to honor their loved ones this way.

CHAPTER EIGHT
Resisting Physician-Assisted Killing as Communities and Institutions

Recall a key line from the introduction to this book: This is an all-hands-on-deck moment that requires an all-of-the-above approach — from our social justice ministries (sometimes identified with the Left or the progressive) to our pro-life ministries (sometimes identified with the Right or the conservative) and beyond.

Happily, as we have seen, fighting for appropriate care for the sick, the disabled, and the dying — and refusing to use physician-assisted killing as a response — has not (yet) been coded "Right" or "Left" politically. It is not a "conservative" position, nor is it a "progressive" one. Indeed, in the United States, we've seen very progressive states refuse to pass PAK for many years in a row — and we saw conservative Republicans take opposition to it out of their platform for the 2024 election cycle. This is also true in Europe, where support or opposition doesn't fall along progressive or conservative battle lines. This is a great gift, for it makes it so much easier for a wide range of Church communities and institutions to contribute to an all-hands-on-deck, all-of-the-above approach to the problems and issues that have led us to the brink of the normalization of PAK.

Obviously, the stakes could not be higher. Indeed, the very notion of human dignity itself is up for grabs. The following two principles that have been guiding our reflections are under direct attack from our consumerist throwaway culture:

- Human life is good for its own sake; the fundamental dignity and equal value of every human life come from being made in the image and likeness of God, not from some capacity for this or that trait.
- Human beings are inherently finite, dependent, and social creatures; this means that we must reject the harmful illusions that we are autonomous individuals who can somehow overcome our finitude.

What are we willing to do to fight for these true ideas — ideas that are at the center of so much of who we are and the culture we have built? Of the very notion of human equality? Of the dignity of the poor, of the sick, of the disabled, and of other marginalized groups? Are we willing to stick out and seem odd in their defense? Are we willing to make sure our current institutions are free and able to live out the truth of these ideas? Are we willing to create new institutions to better defend and live out the truth of these ideas?

As we've seen throughout this book, the issues involved in resisting PAK are so wide-ranging and systemic that it may be difficult to imagine how we can meaningfully respond. Sure, we've just seen how individuals and families can do some very good and important things — especially if they have the financial and other resources to do so — but the broader issues are structural in nature. These kinds of problems are especially difficult if, as our principles tell us, we must have a preferential option for the poor, the least among us, who bear the Holy Face of Christ in a special way. But here's a beautiful thing: The Church has communities and institutions in the United States and around the world that can mobilize on many levels and within many kinds of structures. From our state and national lobbying groups that have an impact on legislation, to our massive health-care system, to an untold number of ministries in our parishes and dioceses, to our state and national bishops' conferences: We can do it!

And whereas this chapter outlines some important ways in which these communities and institutions can respond, many of you reading this book are closer to the actual local needs of your communities — and to the institutions that can respond to them — and thus you will undoubtedly have your own ideas. Act on them. Take the initiative. We will need your creative thinking and activism as part of our all-hands-on-deck response to problems so deeply embedded in our culture.

Securing Government Aid and Support

Whether it is through our Catholic charities groups, our pro-life groups, our health-care systems, or our state and national bishops' conferences, the Church has a very wide range of politically and ideologically diverse options for engaging local, state, and national politicians to achieve some of the structural changes we need in order to support the goals of good lives and good deaths that resist physician-assisted killing.

This book has discussed at length the advantages of aging

and even dying at home. The Pontifical Academy for Life has also explicitly made this case:

> In the light of these considerations, nursing homes should be redeveloped into a socio-health "continuum," i.e. offer some of their services directly in the homes of the elderly: hospitalization at home, taking care of the single person with low or high-intensity assistance responses based on personal needs, where integrated social and health care and home care services are the pivot of a new and modern paradigm.[1]

Some of this will require health care and other kinds of care facilities and systems — including Catholic systems (see below) — to pivot to a home-based model for services. But other structures must also be changed. Regulation of insurance companies must change to allow for and even encourage good coverage and reimbursement rates for this kind of home-based care. But failing these kinds of regulations, or for those who do not have access to insurance so equipped, it seems clear that getting the kind of care we've seen as necessary will require significant resources. Certified nursing assistants, in-home nursing care, specialized equipment, and the like are not cheap — especially if caregivers are paid a living and just wage.

Significantly, lots of people have been thinking about this problem and how to address it. The Senate's special committee on aging has been trying to think through Medicaid funding for these resources. The 2024 Republican platform claims that they will "shift resources back to at-home Senior Care, overturn disincentives that lead to Care Worker shortages, and support unpaid Family Caregivers through Tax Credits and reduced red tape."[2] The Harris campaign for president made in-home eldercare a central part of its platform. Many pro-family and pro-life and social justice groups also support moving in this direction. Perhaps the most common critique of moving in this direction points to cost. In an era in which we have the newly formed Department of Government Efficiency, does it really make sense to create this new and very large entitlement? Well, it turns out that this kind of move toward home-based care would actually *save* taxpayers money.[3] Indeed, for every person Medicaid funds in a nursing home, it can fund three people via home-based care. Having such help inside the home would also free up those who want or need to go back to work. At the same time, more large companies should be regulated and forced to offer paid family leave to care for family members in these situations as well. This should be understood as a basic human right.

Another important and related cause for which Catholic institutions should lobby is access to affordable and appropriate housing. This is essential on a number of levels and important for its own sake (access to affordable housing, according to Catholic teaching, is a basic human right),[4] and it has a direct impact on the two-income trap that causes so many to be unable to properly care for their loved ones, including their elderly loved ones. Subsidies and grants should be made available, as well, for renovations in the home that make this kind of caring easier. Wheelchair ramps, stair lifts, accessible bathrooms and showers, and so forth should be available and affordable to those who need them.

Finally — and we will speak more about care homes and hospices (especially those run by the Church) in more detail below — we need lobbying efforts to make reform of current care homes and hospices practicable. They need to be able to hire enough staff and pay the staff a living wage. They need to be able to have facilities and programs that allow residents to live fully human lives — in relationship with each other, nature, the local community, and so on. And they must not slouch toward robot care. Governmental regulations of such homes, and of insurance reimbursement, can and should be moved to affect these changes. And Catholic lobbying arms must demand this.

Remember, these are just a few of many possible ideas. Again, you are closer to your own particular and local situations and will know what you need. Work with your local organizations to advocate for getting those needs met.

The Response of Catholic Health Care

Responding to the example and call of Christ to care for the sick, the Catholic Church (as we have seen many times throughout this book) has made health care a centerpiece of her ministry. Today the Church is the largest nongovernmental provider of health care in the world, delivering about a quarter of health care worldwide.[5] In the United States, one in seven patients are served in a Catholic facility; the Church operates about seven hundred hospitals and more than sixteen hundred continuing-care clinical facilities.[6] Catholic health care is so prevalent in the United States, especially in poor areas with underserved populations, that some secular folks worry that Catholic institutions (inspired by Catholic values) are the only ones serving these populations.[7]

Catholic health-care institutions, therefore, are remarkably well placed to address some of the structural problems that we've seen need to be addressed. Indeed, if Catholic health-care institutions — including very large health systems — decided to refocus energy on home services and home-care visits, that would be enough by itself to shift a very significant portion of health-care delivery overall. The Ethical and Religious Directives (rules that make sure that Catholic health care authentically reflects its mission) should be changed to foster this important shift, but there is nothing stopping any Catholic institution from making this a priority immediately.

And remember the remarkable fact that Dr. Brescia shared: that his hospice is able to control pain in every instance? While it is true that, again, physical pain doesn't make the top five reasons people request PAK, we do still need to address both the public perception that this is the central problem and the actual cases in which people do not have access to institutions like Calvary Hospital. More support for (and creation of) institutions offering nonviolent medical interventions designed to treat the pain and suffering of patients without killing them must, therefore, be an even stronger focus for Catholic health-care institutions.

A major reason why more sick and dying patients don't get access is because, as Michael Connelly points out in *The Journey's End*, both hospice and palliative care are often disconnected from the rest of the health-care system.[8] Catholic institutions and systems must do more to make sure these options — including (again) home-care options for hospice and palliative care — are carefully integrated into their broader care plans. Connelly also offers us some rich stories indicating the social and interpersonal complexities of entrusting loved ones to even a good hospice program. Catholic health-care institutions, particularly through a robust chaplaincy program, should be putting whole-person care at the foundation of their entire care plans.

One of the central problems that Connelly is keen to point out is that of fragmented health care. The fee-for-service payment system, coupled with hyperspecialization, which divides the human person up into component physical parts, does a disservice to health care generally, but it is especially bad for those who are reaching their final stages of life. Especially if someone entering this stage has chronic disease, he or she can fall through the cracks of our hyperspecialized, medicalized, technologized, we're-in-the-business-of-fixing-organic-problems health-care system. Catholic care systems, however, are uniquely positioned to focus on care for the whole person in the fullness of who he or she is, especially in the final stages of life, when what's often called for is managing a series of problems that cannot, in fact, be fixed.

Connelly notes that the role of the primary care provider and the geriatrician are important here in coordinating care with this whole-person focus, but residencies and fellowships in these areas are attracting comparatively little interest from medical students — with the result that we don't have nearly the workforce necessary to meet this need. Catholic health systems and other institutions, therefore, must get creative in resisting care fragmentation and instead find new ways to coordinate care of the whole person through the entire medical team. Physicians, chaplains, nurses, medical assistants, social workers, ethicists, and the like need to be marshaled in a team-wide attempt to care for residents and patients in the fullness of who they are. Physical, social, and spiritual aspects should all be included directly in the care plan as a matter of course.

Finally, Catholic health systems and other institutions must gear up for the significant legal battles that are undoubtedly coming over PAK. Going back to the first century, we know that our faith resisted the violence of the day (see, in particular, the *Didache*'s prohibition of abortion and infanticide), and we've seen that kind of resistance time and time again throughout our history — not least with German Catholics who resisted the Nazi euthanasia program aimed at *Lebensunwertes Leben*, or "lives unworthy of life." Like those heroic resisters, those who make up today's Catholic health-care institutions must never aim at the death of the patient. As the Bavarian bishops did during the Nazi rule, our bishops must rise up in defense of today's vulnerable populations at risk for PAK. And the Church must — relentlessly and without fail — insist on our religious freedom to provide whole-person, nonviolent care for the most vulnerable. It is difficult to imagine a more necessary vision of care to keep alive.

As we saw earlier in this book, the pressures to engage in PAK will be particularly acute as the dementia crisis unfolds. Yes, it is essential that Catholic health-care institutions never participate in such violence, but it may be even more important for the Church to help create a counterculture of encounter and hospitality that can resist the discarding of these populations. And these institutions will almost certainly be our parishes and dioceses.

Responses of Parishes and Dioceses

It has almost become a cliché, at least in the U.S. Catholic world, to long for the days in which the Catholic parish — led and supported by the local bishop and his diocesan staff — served as a place of genuine community, a real home, a place of genuine encounter and hospitality. In short, our parishes should be the lived reality of two key principles guiding our reflections in this book:

- In both living and dying, the parish should be a place of supportive, real, embodied community — on multiple levels of need (material, social, spiritual).
- The parish should embrace a counterculture of encounter and hospitality as the antidote to our consumerist throwaway culture, which hides and (often violently) discards those whose dignity is inconvenient for the powerful.

Too often — especially as the ties that bind families and neighborhoods together more generally have frayed — our local parish functions as little more than a dispenser of sacraments. As important as the sacraments are, they are meant to take place and take root within the living Body of Christ, the Church, which is a community of the people of God, our brothers and sisters in Christ — a real family!

Not having this community is not a new problem, of course.

Thus the cliché. We have been thinking about how to address it for multiple generations now. The bigger problem, as just suggested, may have less to do with the Church and more to do with the general cultural trends toward isolation and individualism — problems that have shown up time and time again in this book. But the current emergent moment that led to the writing of this book provokes us in a different way, in a new way, in a way that offers us a unique set of opportunities to meet the signs of the times by focusing again on becoming a real community.

Remember the call from the Pontifical Academy for Life for home-based care? Well, the academy also acknowledges that not everyone will be able to make this work, and thus it spends some significant time arguing for a reform of care homes:

> All this makes even more evident the need to support families who, especially if they are made up of just a few children and grandchildren, cannot bear alone, in a home, the sometimes wearisome responsibility of caring for a loved one with a demanding disease that is burdensome in terms of energy and money. A wider network of solidarity must be reinvented, not necessarily and exclusively based on blood ties, but on affiliations, friendships, common feeling, mutual generosity in responding to the needs of all. The decline in social relationships particularly affects the elderly. As they age and important physical and mental frailties emerge, they are missing points of reference, people to rely on for all the problems of their lives.[9]

Added to this should be the particular context of our dementia crisis. Recall the special danger PAK poses for this population: Our care homes are already overburdened, and we've seen how high percentages of residents with dementia in nursing homes are given dangerous "chemical straitjackets" to keep them docile. But as bad as this is right now, if current trends continue, the number of people with dementia will double in twenty years and triple in thirty years. What will our care system look like then if nothing changes?[10] Recall the way that I suggested those faced with this kind of disease will feel:

> How would you feel if, next year, as will happen for millions and millions in the consumerist West, you were given an early-onset-dementia diagnosis? What if ... you saw a future in which you would be removed from your home, isolated in an institution, engaged primarily by robot "caregivers" and "friends," given substandard treatment and care, and be dependent on others to bear your burdens? What if you knew that you would very rarely see your family or friends, go to church, or otherwise engage with your community? What if it was likely that you would eventually be given a "chemical straitjacket" and forget the names of your loved ones? What if this would also cost you, your spouse, your family, and perhaps our social safety nets a ton of money?

Embarrassingly, secular institutions are doing a much better job of responding to this aspect of the dementia crisis. Consider the mission statement of institutions such as Glenner Town Square:

> Our mission is to provide affordable and accessible adult day care and support services to families affected by Alzheimer's and other forms of memory impairment diseases. We do this by providing innovative adult day care programs, family support, case management, crisis intervention, family and community education, advocacy, information and referrals.[11]

So much of what we've discussed is addressed by this mission! And take a look at this list of specifics offered to those whom Glenner cares for:

- Loved one continues to live at home
- Nurse (RN/LVN) on-site during operating hours
- Medication management
- Dementia-specific activities
- Brain-fit exercises
- Music therapy
- Pet therapy
- 5:1 participant-to-direct care staff ratio
- Safe, secure, family-like environment
- Socialization and stimulation
- Professionally-facilitated caregiver support groups
- Transportation assistance
- Private pay, long term care insurance, and VA benefits accepted
- Full-day and half-day rates available ($100 full-day/$70 half-day)
- Two meals included in full-day rate
- Physical & occupational therapy
- Reminiscence therapy[12]

Reminiscence therapy may be the most interesting aspect of the care Glenner offers: The "town square" space has been created to look like a town in the 1950s, including things like a diner, a hospital, a movie theater, a museum, a library, and even a pet store — complete with fish and visiting dogs.[13] All is designed, beautifully and carefully, to look like the life that many of today's dementia-affected people remember from their teens, twenties, and thirties. Could the Church enact her own version of this kind of outreach, geared in a similarly specific and intentional way to a particularly vulnerable population, that locates them within a real community in a way that helps them thrive? The answer is yes, but we would need the right leadership. Especially in light of the recent biopic from Angel Studies, the life and influence of St. Frances Xavier Cabrini has received significantly more attention in the last couple of years. Her life's witness was to shape her religious order to focus on the crisis of desperate immigrant populations. We need leaders inspired by her example to lead in similar ways to focus on the dementia crisis.[14] These leaders should be equipped by bishops' conferences, bishops, and their diocesan staffs to build a new "empire of hope" — but this time for the elderly, the disabled, the sick, and the dying. Cabrini founded nearly seventy institutions, including housing structures and hospitals, several of which were created from repurposed buildings. We need a number of Cabrinis today to show similarly bold leadership in addressing a culture in crisis — indeed, a culture on the brink of turning to mass killing via PAK.

And, as good as they are, the Church can go beyond the Glenner Family Centers of the world, which meet only the physical and social needs of the people they serve. The Church can address their spiritual needs too! And as more and more dementia residents and other folks with memory issues remember the 1960s more than they do the 1950s, the Church has a number of facilities and physical spaces available that could be repurposed in such a way: empty or leased school buildings that were built in the 1960s. After decades of school closures, how many of these could become, say, a "St. Joe's Drop-In Center" — with traditional classroom learning, arts and crafts, gym, library, lunch, recess outside (with work and strolls in the garden), and, importantly, time in the church or chapel?

Here's another idea: What about the many empty rectories and convents that have become available for repurposing as we have far fewer women religious and priests, along with many more parish mergers? Some have already taken the lead in converting these into affordable care homes.[15] But these may not be centers of real community, and despite better-than-average caregiving, many continue to suffer from the problems of isolation that we've seen throughout this book. But what about remodeling these buildings in ways that — like the drop-in centers mentioned above — would turn them into real communities of people? What about adding a bar that local parishioners might frequent, say, to get a drink on their way home from work and interact with the residents and the staff? Or as part of "Vespers and Vino," a tradition beloved by the Los Angeles Carmelites? What about having a large projection area where a wide variety of folks would gather for movie or game nights? What about having one or two parish daily Masses at this facility's chapel? What about book clubs, board games, and music and theatrical performances? It could be a crossroads of the parish community!

And think about this: Many (perhaps most) of these repurposed schools, convents, and rectories still exist on parishes' physical campuses. This provides all kinds of opportunities for local parish members (including confirmation candidates!) to drop in and volunteer. This would not only keep costs down but, again, could contribute to the flourishing of a real community. The children from a still-functioning school or a religious-education program could make regular trips to the facility to eat, talk, watch movies, and worship with residents — creating a community that is genuinely intergenerational. It is well known that our current secular structures and technologies have produced both older and younger generations that are very often isolated and alone, depressed and anxious, and in desperate need of these kinds of real encounters. These parishes could be not only real communities but genuine ecosystems of Christ-centered love.

The Pontifical Academy for Life explicitly invokes this kind of intergenerational vision by recalling the Gospel account of the Presentation of the Lord in the Temple, an event that is sometimes called the "Feast of the Encounter" in the Eastern churches. It writes:

> On that occasion, in fact, two elderly people, Simeon and Anna, meet the Child Jesus: two frail elderly reveal him to the world as the light of the people and speak of him to those who were waiting for the fulfillment of the divine promises (cf. Lk 2:32–38). Simeon takes Jesus in his arms: the Child and the elderly mutually support each other as if to symbolize the beginning and the end of earthly existence: in fact, as some liturgical hymns proclaim, "the old man carried the Child, but the Child supported the elderly person." Hope thus springs from the encounter between two fragile people, a child and an elderly person, to remind us, in our times that exalt the culture of performance and strength, that the Lord loves to reveal greatness in smallness and strength in tenderness.

And before you dismiss this as pie-in-the-sky nonsense dreamed up by people who clearly don't live in the real world, consider that this kind of thing *is already happening*. Consider The Pillars, a child and eldercare center in Minnesota, for instance.[16] The childcare center is on the ground floor of a building that also houses and cares for seniors. Or, as the staff puts it, "Grandfriends are upstairs, and sometimes some live downstairs." The older adults encounter the children in multiple ways: reading stories, holding and feeding babies, helping water the plants in the garden, and sometimes just free playing.

This is good for the older adults for a host of reasons that should by now be obvious, but it is also very good for the children. Indeed, these encounters change the kids in profound ways. Parents report their children getting "a sense of confidence" from these interactions — along with a new attitude "of fun and playfulness." In addition, these interactions help the kids connect to older adults more generally and see them as a population firmly within their social circles, instead of one pushed out to the margins that they rarely encounter. A parent who has a four-year-old and one-year-old cared for at The Pillars said: "Every time we go out [to] the grocery stores or something, they're like, 'Oh, Mom, look, there's a grandfriend.' ... Or they're like, 'She looks like grandfriend Launa,' like someone in a wheelchair. So it just brings a great awareness to my kids that they can see these grandfriends are also their friends."[17]

A Change of Heart

Many more ideas could be offered here, of course. Catholic parishes and other institutions should be focused on resisting ableism and ageism in all its forms; among other things, this means bringing and welcoming disabled children and adults to church and other public activities associated with our institutions. Also, and especially as the sources of dementia and some of these other illnesses are better understood, we should find ways to move our Catholic institutions (and especially our Catholic schools) to address their root causes. Significantly, these root causes look more and more like poor diets and poor levels of activity — both of which can be addressed in several other Catholic contexts, particularly our schools.

As mentioned above, we need the creativity of you, the reader, to think and pray more about what else could be done.

But in closing the book here, it might be appropriate to take our focus off saving the lives of those at risk for physician-assisted killing. This may seem like a strange way to end, especially given that this concern has driven everything about the book to this point. But in a Catholic context, morality is not just about the other; it is about who we — the agents — are as well. Just as the more we hurt others, the more we hurt ourselves — the more we help others flourish, the more we flourish ourselves.[18] When we live out the Gospel, our hearts are changed from hearts of stone to hearts of flesh.

Think about how many millions are trapped in a self-centered, isolated throwaway culture that offers little more than addictive, self-destructive, technologized consumerism. How many millions are vocationally frustrated, mortally lonely, and generally (and perhaps even desperately) looking for meaning in their lives? How many yearn for the change of heart the Gospel offers?

Is it outrageous to think that millions of lukewarm or fallen-away Christians of various stripes will come to be deeply troubled by this fact and, faced with the cultural emergency described in this book, will come to grips with the importance of the faith of their fathers for the broader culture in which they live? Wouldn't the millions of human beings with late-stage dementia, at risk of being discarded, also tug at the spiritual heartstrings of those who are more traditional believers but not very active in living out their faith? And wouldn't the massive mobilization efforts suggested above be similarly attractive to new converts to the Faith? What energy, what hope, such a movement could bring! How much it could build! How many it could serve! How many hearts it could change! It could truly be the light of Christ shining in the darkness.

Indeed, in joining the ranks of those resisting PAK, the life you most clearly save may be your own.

APPENDIX 1
Principles and Prayers

Human life is good for its own sake; the fundamental dignity and equal value of every human life comes from being made in the image and likeness of God, not because of some capacity for this or that trait.

Human beings are inherently finite, dependent, and social creatures; this means that we must reject the harmful illusions that we are autonomous individuals who can somehow overcome our finitude.

We must consistently keep our death front of mind, such that it fundamentally shapes how we live — both in this life and with an eye to the next.

We must give up on the harmful illusions of autonomy and control that lead to the idolatrous extremes of (1) fighting for extended life at any cost and (2) responding to dying by taking death into one's own hands — both of which misunderstand the dignity of the human person.

We should resist death when appropriate but also discern the time to accept and even welcome death as a gift from God (as part of a choice about how to live, rather than as a choice to die).

In both living and dying, a supportive, real, embodied community — on multiple levels of need (material, social, spiritual) — holds central importance.

We must focus on a counterculture of encounter and hospitality as the antidote to our consumerist throwaway culture, which hides and (often violently) discards those whose dignity is inconvenient for the powerful.

We must be willing to show true compassion — to suffer with the suffering. And when we suffer, we should see this not as heaping burdens on others but, rather, as part of the give-and-take that comes with living in a true community, in which we give others opportunities to love.

We must always look through a lens that gives special priority to the most vulnerable, the least among us, those who bear the Holy Face of Christ in a special way: the poor, the disabled, the widow and the orphan, the racial minority — and, of course, the aging, the sick, and the dying.

Prayers

Memento Mori
Jesus, when I take my last breath, may you be on my mind and in my heart. Amen.

Saint Joseph
O glorious Saint Joseph, I choose you today for my special patron in life and at the hour of my death. Preserve and increase in me the spirit of prayer and fervor in the service of God. Remove far from me every kind of sin; obtain for me that my death may not come upon me unawares, but that I may have time to confess my sins sacramentally and to bewail them with a most perfect understanding and a most sincere and perfect contrition, in order that I may breathe forth my soul into the hands of Jesus and Mary. Amen.

From St. Francis of Assisi's "Canticle of the Creatures"
Praised be You, my Lord, through our Sister Bodily Death,
from whom no one living can escape.
    Woe to those who die in mortal sin.
Blessed are those whom death will find in Your most holy will,
for the second death shall do them no harm.
    Praise and bless my Lord and give Him thanks
and serve Him with great humility.

Prayer of Surrender from St. Ignatius of Loyola
Take, Lord, and receive all my liberty, my memory, my understanding, and my entire will, all I have and call my own. You have given all to me. To you, Lord, I return it. Everything is yours; do with it what you will. Give me only your love and your grace; that is enough for me.

St. Teresa of Ávila's "Bookmark"

Let nothing disturb you. Let nothing frighten you, all things are passing away. God never changes. Patience obtains all things. Whoever has God lacks nothing. God alone suffices.

APPENDIX 2
Practical Guidance

Include the relevant players (children, pastors, neighbors, siblings, friends, and so forth) early on — that is, *right now*, if you haven't already.

Talk to the relevant players about your preferences. Designate a life-affirming medical proxy (LAMP) with whom to have detailed discussions and share legal and other documents. (See below.) Share copies of these documents broadly, keep electronic copies, keep originals in a very safe place, and make sure the right people know where they are.

Make sure to get a clinical "quarterback" for all your medical care and to coordinate with specialists. This could be your primary care provider (PCP) or your geriatrician. This person should be very aware of your preferences and values and should share them.

Make sure you have a spiritual team at the ready as well. If you can, be treated at a Catholic hospital that has the reputation of taking the Church's teaching and Ethical and Religious Directives (ERDs) seriously. Explore what sort of religious resources (chaplains, chapels, visiting options for priests, pastors, and so forth) the hospital offers.

Discuss these matters in some detail with your pastor, including your preferred funeral and burial arrangements. See if you can work with your pastor to create or increase support for a ministry that would be a home for parish conversations, information, talks, projects, and other supports for those in these situations. This should include prayer teams, meal trains, and perhaps even project managers for some of the ideas in this book.

Get familiar with the lingo, practices, and options based on your situation. Do not be intimidated in the face of modern medicine and its practitioners: Look up information on your illness or condition and read what journals say about treatments. Knowledge is indeed power, and in vulnerable conditions with a loss of control, this power is essential. We typically spend more time on research for the purchase of a home or a car than we do on medical care. This time and attention should be inverted.

Armed with this knowledge, be polite, but always *stand up for yourself and your family members*. Know your rights and options. If at a Catholic hospital, hold the hospital accountable to the ERDs. Stand your ground and do not be intimidated. This is easier when there is some time to prepare; it is more difficult in an emergency. For instance, what may begin as a life-saving situation may end up cascading into life support or life-sustaining care, resulting in a different moral calculus every five minutes. Even standing your ground is going to be hard when you're sinking in quicksand. All the more reason to prepare well.

Legal Stuff

Get close to a lawyer you may have in your family or social circles. Or consider investing in a monthly prepaid legal plan, so you will have legal help available if you need it — as it's very possible you will.

Both the National Catholic Bioethics Center and the Catholic Medical Association (see "Trustworthy Catholic Resources" below) have strong reservations against having a general Practitioner Orders for Life-Sustaining Treatment (POLST) form. Instead, here are two good forms to consider using:

- A Catholic Health Care Directive: https://ndcatholic.org/chd/resources/NDdirective2023.pdf
- Five Wishes: https://www.fivewishes.org/five-wishes-sample.pdf

Beyond these forms, try to think about every potential situation you can imagine and talk about it with several others. It's also a good idea to find a place to write it down.

You may want to think about instructions for household things while your health is compromised: pet care, yard maintenance, plants, indoor care, housesitting, and so on. Your wishes should already be in the above document, but you may need to give instructions as to how to do each thing.

These forms and documents and conversations should be combined with having a very clearly established medical power of attorney who is explicitly designated a life-affirming medical proxy (LAMP).

- Here is a general LAMP form: https://halovoice.org/wp-content/uploads/LAMP-Form-1.pdf.
- Here is a form with specific Catholic language: https://macatholic.org/wpcontent/uploads/2022/10/MCC-HCP-2016.pdf.
- Legal forms for after one's death are also important. Living wills, for instance, focus on what will be the plan for your money and other goods after your death. Here, best practices include finding a durable power of attorney for finance. Each state has different requirements. Here's a good source to learn more about specifics where you live: https://www.justia.com/estateplanning/power-of-attorney/power-of-attorney-laws-50-state-survey/.
- It may also be the case that you want to plan out what happens with your *digital* estate, such as your email and social media accounts. Here's a nice resource for that: https://www.fastcompany.com/91228523/why-you-need-a-digital-estate-plan-and-how-to-create-one.
- Consider getting your finances into a trust in order to make some of the care you'll need (see below) more affordable.

Clinical Red Flags and Options for Responding

Again, (1) educate yourself, (2) have documents and conversations ready, and (3) stand your ground when it comes to your values and making sure they are reflected in your medical care or a loved one's. Get as much of your common understanding as you can in writing. Even when you do these things, it can often be difficult to know what is happening in particular clinical-medical contexts, especially since some medical professionals can be very good at achieving the result they want on the sly. Here are some ways to find out about clinical red flags:

- Pay close attention to how the clinical team describes various matters. If they are consistently at odds with your research, that is a red flag.
- Research the institution to see whether it has any history of being sued or otherwise challenged related to matters that are important to you.
- See if you can find any evidence or history of "slow coding" or "show coding" — a situation in which a person or family wants "full code" (everything done), but the medical team only pretends to do so and instead refuses to offer certain care in order to bring about death.
- See if you can find any evidence or history of overtreatment, particularly in research-centered hospitals where there is added pressure to try new, boundary-pushing, or experimental treatments.
- Pay close attention to how well you are being listened to. Are people giving you eye contact or merely concerned about entering things into a computer?
- Pay close attention to how various folks react to the Ethical and Religious Directives. Are they interested and proud to honor them, or do they explicitly or implicitly find them something to be ignored, sidestepped, or overcome?
- Be careful about being steered into a do-not-resuscitate order that you do not want. You or your loved one may be at special risk if there is a significant disability involved. Also, be sure that the medical team is very clear about contexts in which you'd want aggressive treatment and other contexts in which you may not. There are various options: full code versus chemical code only (no intubation, defibrillation, but any and all medications as needed) versus no code. Be clear

about the details. It is a red flag if health-care professionals demand an either-or situation.
- Be careful about being steered in the direction of rejecting food and water via a gastric tube. This is not a medical treatment but is part of basic care for every human being and should not be rejected except in very, very unusual circumstances. Be careful about being steered in the direction of food and water in a more general way.
- Also be careful about being steered in the direction of receiving more and more morphine — not as a way of treating pain, but as a way of aiming at death by making it come faster.
- If it is your loved one who is dying, you can be with that loved one throughout the process, even outside normal visiting hours, especially if you are the LAMP and the patient needs you to advocate for him or her. It is a red flag if someone tries to get you to leave.

Here are some options for responses if you sense something may be wrong:

- Build close relationships with your nurses. They very often know what is going on behind the scenes, and engaging with them is a very good first step. You can say things such as "They aren't listening to us" or "Are there any other resources you would recommend here for us?" Nurses can be allies in interacting with physicians and bending the ears of the broader medical team.
- Nurses can also recommend and help call ethics consultants or involve chaplains and patient-care ombudsmen, the patient-relations line or office, the

local ethics committee, or the health equity service at your hospital. You can also work on your own to access these resources. In fact, it is a good idea to research in advance procedures for doing this.
- You can go outside the local system and file complaints with medical boards, go to Catholic oversight organizations (such as your priest or pastor; the local diocese or bishop, ethics VP, and ethics committees for the larger Catholic health system; and the Catholic Medical Association).

Finding Resources: Home Care, Care Homes, and Hospices

As we have seen in this book, we need to find far better ways to help those without the necessary resources to find good in-home care and (when necessary) good care homes and hospices. Still, there are important ideas and resources to consider here.

First, an overall recommendation and reminder: Do your research (sometimes in unexpected places, such as parish bulletin ads!) and *ask around in your local context*. When researching, talk to as many people as possible about their experiences, including social workers (off the record). Ask them about services and facilities to consider and those to avoid. When interviewing someone or visiting a facility, ask clear and even pointed questions with regard to your most important concerns.

Home Care Resources
- Check out the American Academy of Home Care Medicine. It offers lots of good information on specific services and how to get them, including home-based primary care: https://www.aahcm.org/what_is_hbpc.
- Home care can include primary care physicians,

nurse practitioners, physician assistants, nurses, social workers, emergency medical technicians, pharmacists, and more.
- Some states reimburse home-based care through Medicaid. Medicare covers it in part. The VA has it. It is important to investigate these and other local resources. For instance, some states (such as Pennsylvania, currently) allow you to route disability care to home-care nursing, whereas others (such as Maryland, currently) do not. This means that you need to do your homework.
- The Center for Medicaid and Medicaid Services also offers significant information on resources and funding: https://www.cms.gov/training-education/partner-outreach-resources/american-indian-alaska-native/ltss-ta-center/information/ltss-models/home-and-community-based-services.
- Here's a nice resource on various ways to find in-home care (this resource is specific to Michigan, but the principles and approaches found here work across many states): https://www.rightathome.net/mid-michigan/resources/guides/ways-to-pay.
- The AARP offers a number of good resources, including advice for hiring an in-home caregiver: https://www.aarp.org/caregiving/home-care/info-2018/hiring-caregiver.html.
- Also, take a look at your local "aging adult resource center" — almost every county has one.

Care Homes, Palliative Care, and Hospice

- Asking around for your local context is incredibly important. Start now doing your research and becoming familiar with what is available to you.

Sometimes difficult health events can happen very quickly, and it is good to have plans already in place.
- Many of the same resources above can be used to explore options for care homes, palliative care, and hospices when the time is right, but the focus should be on in-home care options first.
- Think about institutions that are run explicitly in a Catholic context. Those run by the Carmelites and the Little Sisters of the Poor are proven winners, obviously, and Calvary Hospice Hospital is the gold standard, but not everyone has access to these great institutions. Think about those run by Catholic Charities and others who may have commitments to a Catholic vision of the good. But be sure to ask questions of them in this regard when doing your research.
- Be sure to ask pointed questions of institutions you are considering. Visit them often, perhaps at unexpected times. Talk to as many people as you can who work there. Talk to those, again, who have experience with family, friends, and neighbors who have been cared for there.
- If in-home care is not an option and you must choose a care facility for your loved one, let them know you will be visiting often — but don't always tell them when you are coming. Try to visit at various times where and when you can get an authentic sense of what's going on there.
- Here is a good Catholic resource for planning for palliative care in a Catholic context (this is from the Archdiocese of Boston, but again, the principles and approaches found here would work in many contexts): https://bostoncatholic.org/resources-for

-palliative-care-and-advance-care-planning.

Trustworthy Catholic Resources

Samaritanus Bonus, the Dicastery for the Doctrine of the Faith's Statement on Care for Persons in Critical and Terminal Phases of Life, https://press.vatican.va/content/salastampa/en/bollettino/pubblico/2020/09/22/200922a.html.

The Ethical and Religious Directives for Catholic Health Care Services, 6th edition, 2018, part 5: "Issues in Care for the Seriously Ill and Dying," https://www.usccb.org/about/doctrine/ethical-and-religious-directives/upload/ethical-religious-directives-catholic-health-service-sixth-edition-2016-06.pdf.

"To Live Each Day with Dignity," the United States Bishops' policy statement on assisted suicide, 2011, https://www.usccb.org/issues-and-action/human-life-and-dignity/assisted-suicide/to-live-each-day/upload/to-live-each-day-with-dignity-hyperlinked.pdf.

Miscellaneous official Catholic Church teachings, fact sheets, and more, https://www.usccb.org/prolife/assisted-suicide-euthanasia.

State-by-state resources, https://www.catholicendoflife.org/resources/.

Catholic Medical Association, https://www.cathmed.org/assets/files/POLST_Paradigm_and_Form.pdf.

Caring for the Whole Person (California Catholic Conference), https://wholeperson.care/.

Catholic Psychotherapy Association (mental health issues often arise for both the individual and the family), https://cpa.ce21.com/directory.

APPENDIX 3
Responses to FAOs (Frequently Articulated Objections)

Objection One: Isn't it a basic human right to have autonomous control over one's life and body, and also one's death — even if it requires physician-assisted killing?

The idea that we have absolute individual autonomous control over our lives and bodies is an illusion — as the experiences of illness, disability, and death indicate. In addition, when we pretend that everyone has such autonomy, it works out especially poorly for those who most obviously do not have such autonomy. We end up creating a situation in which vulnerable populations are explicitly or structurally coerced into deaths they don't want. The sick, the disabled, and the dying are devalued. Offering PAK also requires pressuring health-care institutions and workers to violate their own vision of their profession and forcing them to think of killing others as a way of offering them health care.

Objection Two: What about religious freedom? What right does anyone have to force onto others his or her religious belief related to PAK? Especially when it comes to incredibly intimate values related to how to live and how to die?

There is no such thing as a neutral "view from nowhere" that is purely rational and objective when it comes to the values and questions at the heart of the debates over PAK. Secular people also bring their own visions of the good, with first principles for which they do not have arguments. For instance, a lot of secular utilitarians believe in PAK because it fits with their first principle to "maximize pleasure and minimize pain for everyone." (As we've seen, they are wrong even on this narrow point.) If you ask such people why they believe this principle, it is clear their belief is based on intuition, authority, or some other kind of secular faith. Everyone reasons morally from these kinds of first principles, and the results of debates over PAK policy cannot help but impose certain first principles and visions of the good onto other, contradictory, first principles and visions of the good. There is no reason to artificially exclude religious people from the debate in this regard.

Objection Three: Isn't it cruel to force someone to live with terrible pain or a disability if he or she doesn't want to? PAK seems necessary to help people avoid both of these.

With regard to physical pain, we've seen that it doesn't even make the top five reasons people request PAK and that introducing PAK into a society can actually make palliative care worse.

That's at least in part because palliative care (including palliative sedation) can, when used appropriately, control a patient's pain — even in the most difficult circumstances. With regard to disability, it is a terrible message to disabled people to tell them that we can understand why their lives are so awful that they would want to kill themselves. It is usually people with very privileged lives who cannot imagine the value of a disabled life, and we should err on the side of protecting and listening to the most vulnerable. It is disabled populations and economically vulnerable populations who are most skeptical of PAK.

Objection Four: How is palliative care any different from PAK? Doesn't it often result in death in both circumstances? Why should we distinguish between them?

Here, it is very important to think about the intention or object of two different actions and how they are different. With palliative care, one is trying to control pain, and one may foresee but *not* intend that death will be the result. Indeed, one would be thrilled if pain could be controlled without killing the patient or speeding his or her death. With PAK, death is intended as the means to the end being pursued and thus is quite different. By analogy, think about the difference between a terrorist who uses a bomb with the intention of killing innocent people and an honorable bomber pilot who drops bombs foreseeing but not intending that innocent people may be killed. The former individual would be upset if no innocent people were killed in the blast, while the latter would be thrilled. We make this distinction (via the principle of double effect) in many cases, not just when it comes to distinguishing between palliative care and PAK.

Objection Five: Your children and others paying for and otherwise supporting your care and offering in-person care have

lives and goals and dreams quite apart from you. Don't be selfish and put that kind of burden on them. Don't drain them of their cash and time. Use PAK.

We have seen that it is very often parents and older adults who need to get comfortable with the idea of having someone care for them. Too often, they are the ones who discourage their children and others from living close by and living out the privilege of caring for their loved ones. It is not selfish to accept that kind of love and care; rather, it is the way of the world that prioritizes family and the unchosen obligation to honor one's father and mother. The first and primary community that cares for those who are sick, disabled, or dying is the family. And though it is sometimes difficult, it is a life-giving privilege to do so. And we should provide families with the resources to do so.

Objection Six: *The country is broke and in hopeless debt. We cannot afford to outsource our costs of care for the elderly, the sick, and the disabled to future generations, who will be forced to pay off our debt for new social programs. PAK offers this kind of cost savings to future generations.*

Killing the sick and the disabled — some of the most vulnerable people around — in order to save money is one of the worst human rights violations imaginable. Furthermore, as we have seen in this book, using resources to care for people at home is far more efficient than spending the money we do now in the often isolating and dehumanizing care homes and clinics that dominate the current system.

Objection Seven: *Catholics are pro-life, and this means doing everything one can to save and extend life. Anything else would mean acting against the value of human life.*

This could not be further from the truth. Just look at the examples of Jesus and the martyrs: They were faithful to their heavenly Father, even when they foresaw but did not intend that their fidelity would likely lead to their deaths. They showed that, sometimes, it is not only acceptable to not save or extend life — but sometimes, it is quite appropriate and holy to do so. One must never aim at death as one's goal, but neither should one grasp for more life at any cost. This is the very definition of idolatry.

Notes

Introduction: On the Brink of What, Exactly?

1. Noah Cohen, "'It Could Have Been Tragic' Police Say of Dramatic Bridge Rescue," NJ.com, March 29, 2017, https://www.nj.com/essex/2017/03/cops_recount_rescue_of_man_hanging_off_newark_brid.html; "May 2017. Good Samaritans Holding onto a Man Who Wanted to Jump Off a Bridge for Nearly 2 Hours," https://www.reddit.com/r/pics/comments/kuw4r7/may_2017_good_samaritans_holding_onto_a_man_who/.

2. Natasha Lennard, "29-Year-Old Brittany Maynard's Suicide Was Heroic," *Vice*, November 3, 2014, https://www.vice.com/en/article/3kewyb/29-year-old-brittany-maynards-suicide-was-heroic.

3. "Why Do We Keep Severely Mentally Disabled People Alive, Other Than the Fact That They're Human?," Quora, 2025, https://www.quora.com/Why-do-we-keep-severely-mentally-disabled-people-alive-other-than-the-fact-that-theyre-human.

4. John Craven (@johncraven1) post on X, February 27, 2024, https://twitter.com/johncraven1/status/1762585291687096542.

5. Capital News Service, "'It's Certainly Over': Aid-in-Dying Bill Falters in Md. Senate for This Year," *Daily Record*, March 1, 2024, https://thedailyrecord.com/2024/03/01/its-certainly-over-aid-in-dying-bill-falters-in-md-senate-for-this-year/.

6. "Editorial: 'Right to Die' Debate Comes to Illinois. Both Sides Have Merit, But We Would Vote No," *Chicago Tribune*, March 8, 2024, https://www.chicagotribune.com/2024/03/08/editorial-right-to-die-debate-comes-to-illinois-both-sides-have-merit-but-we-would-vote-no/.

7. "Assisted Suicide Bill Fails to Go to Vote After Over 60 Peers Speak in Opposition in 7-Hour Debate," *Right to Life News*, October 22, 2021, https://righttolife.org.uk/news/meacher-assisted-suicide-bill-debate.

8. Wesley J. Smith, "European Court: Assisted Suicide Not a Human Right," *National Review*, June 13, 2024, https://www.nationalreview.com/corner/european-court-assisted-suicide-not-a-human-right/.

9. AAPD (@AAPD) post on X, June 27, 2024, https://x.com/AAPD/status/1806525873194975432.

10. Jonah McKeown, "American Medical Association Retains Opposition to Assisted Suicide," Catholic News Agency, November 14, 2023, https://www.catholicnewsagency.com/news/256012/american-medical-association-retains-opposition-to-assisted-suicide-amid-catholic-doctors-advocacy.

11. Luke Parsnow, "Medical Society of the State of New York Supports Medical Aid in Dying Act," Spectrum News 1, April 15, 2024, https://spectrumlocalnews.com/nys/central-ny/politics/2024/04/15/medical-society-of-the-state-of-new-york-supports-medical-aid-in-dying-act.

12. News Wires, "Macron Backs Bill That Would Allow Medically Assisted Death," France24, October 3, 2024, https://www.france24.com/en/france/20240310-macron-backs-bill-allowing-medically-assisted-death.

13. Anders Koskinen, "MN Muslims and Catholics Join Forces to Fight Assisted Suicide," *Alpha News*, November 24, 2016, https://alphanews.org/mn-muslims-catholics-join-forces-fight-assisted-suicide/.

14. Charles C. Camosy, "Can Secular Health Care Institutions Be Trusted to Make a Moral Brain Death Policy?" Religion News Service, April 29, 2024, https://religionnews.com/2024/04/29/can-secular-health-care-institutions-be-trusted-to-make-a-moral-brain-death-policy/.

15. "Statement from Tyler White," Dignity Denied, December 7, 2020, https://dignitydenied.ca/2020/12/07/statement-from-tyler-white/.

16. "DFCM Welcomes First Chair in End-of-Life Care and Medical Assistance in Dying," Family & Community Medicine, University of Toronto, February 4, 2022, https://dfcm.utoronto.ca/news/dfcm

-welcomes-first-chair-end-life-care-and-medical-assistance-dying.

17. Amanda Achtman (@AmandaAchtman), post on X, April 25, 2022, https://x.com/AmandaAchtman/status/1518546478821789696.

18. Amanda Achtman, "Euthanasia in the Castle: Inside Europe's Museums of Nazi Medical Crimes," *Public Discourse*, October 14, 2024, https://www.thepublicdiscourse.com/2024/10/96127/.

19. Arthur L. Caplan, "Misusing the Nazi Analogy," *Science* 309, no. 3754 (July 22, 2005), https://www.science.org/doi/pdf/10.1126/science.1115437.

20. Ashley K. Fernandes, "Why Did So Many Doctors Become Nazis?" *Tablet*, December 10, 2020, https://www.tabletmag.com/sections/history/articles/fernandes-doctors-who-became-nazis.

21. Ian Dowbiggen, *A Concise History of Euthanasia: Life, Death, God, and Medicine* (Rowman & Littlefield Publishers, 2007).

22. Charles McDaniel, "A Model for Christian Engagement in the Age of 'Consumer Eugenics,'" *Journal of Religion and Society* 22 (2020), https://cdr.creighton.edu/server/api/core/bitstreams/438db0c6-a707-4ae6-8bff-0b6f1e521160/content.

23. Pius XI, *Casti Connubii*, December 31, 1930, Vatican.va, pars. 63, 68.

24. Thaddeus M. Pope, "Medical Aid in Dying," *The Good Death Society Blog*, February 11, 2024, https://www.thegooddeathsocietyblog.net/2024/02/11/medical-aid-in-dying/

Chapter One: What Physician-Assisted Killing Reveals About Our Culture

1. Oregon Public Health Division, "Oregon's Death with Dignity Act — 2014," Oregon Health Authority, 2025, https://www.oregon.gov/oha/ph/ProviderPartnerResources/EvaluationResearch/DeathwithDignityAct/Documents/year17.pdf.

2. Madeline Li, et al., "Medical Assistance in Dying — Implementing a Hospital-Based Program in Canada," *New England Journal of Medicine* 376, no. 21 (May 25, 2017), https://doi.org/10.1056

/NEJMms1700606.

3. Li et al., "Medical Assistance in Dying."

4. Marianne K. Dees et al., "'Unbearable Suffering': A Qualitative Study on the Perspectives of Patients Who Request Assistance in Dying," *Journal of Medical Ethics* 37, no. 12 (December 2011): 727–34, https://doi.org/10.1136/jme.2011.045492; Ezekiel J. Emmanuel et al., "Attitudes and Practices of Euthanasia and Physician-Assisted Suicide in the United States, Canada, and Europe," JAMA 316, no. 1 (July 5, 2016): 79–90, https://doi.org/10.1001/jama.2016.8499.

5. David Albert Jones, "Evidence of Harm: Assessing the Impact of Assisted Dying/Assisted Suicide on Palliative Care," The Anscombe Bioethics Centre, 2024, https://bioethics.org.uk/media/t1bf0icr/evidence-of-harm-assessing-the-impact-of-assisted-dying-assisted-suicide-on-palliative-care-prof-david-albert-jones.pdf.

6. Brian Bird, "Canada Is Not Only Euthanizing Persons but Personhood Itself," *Public Discourse*, December 10, 2023, https://www.thepublicdiscourse.com/2023/12/92075/.

7. Matt Gilmour, "Spina Bifida Patient Says Montreal Hospital Staff Twice Offered MAID Unprompted," CTV News, July 4, 2024, https://www.ctvnews.ca/montreal/article/spina-bifida-patient-says-montreal-hospital-staff-twice-offered-maid-unprompted/.

8. David Baxter, "Medically Assisted Death for Mental Illness Delayed Until 2027: Minister," Global News, February 1, 2024, https://globalnews.ca/news/10265616/maid-expansion-delayed-2027/.

9. Rachel Watts, "Quadriplegic Quebec Man Chooses Assisted Dying After 4-Day ER Stay Leaves Horrific Bedsore," CBC News, April 12, 2024, https://www.cbc.ca/news/canada/montreal/assisted-death-quadriplegic-quebec-man-er-bed-sore-1.7171209.

10. Maria Cheng, "'Disturbing': Experts Troubled by Canada's Euthanasia Laws," Associated Press, August 11, 2022, https://apnews.com/article/covid-science-health-toronto-7c631558a457188d2bd2b5cfd360a867.

11. Ibid.

12. Avis Favaro, "Woman with Chemical Sensitivities Chose Medically-Assisted Death After Failed Bid to Get Better Housing," CTV News, April 13, 2022, https://www.ctvnews.ca/health/woman-with-chemical-sensitivities-chose-medically-assisted-death-after-failed-bid-to-get-better-housing-1.5860579.

13. Charles C. Camosy, "A Glimpse into a Post-Christian Future: Public Support for Killing the Poor and Disabled," *Public Discourse*, June 12, 2023, https://www.thepublicdiscourse.com/2023/06/89216/.

14. Michael Lee, "Canadian Soldier with PTSD 'Outraged' When VA Suggested Euthanasia," *New York Post*, August 22, 2022, https://nypost.com/2022/08/22/canadian-soldier-with-ptsd-outraged-when-va-suggested-euthanasia/; Tom Yun, "Paralympian Trying to Get Wheelchair Ramp Says Veterans Affairs Employee Offered Her Assistance in Dying," CTV News, December 2, 2022, https://www.ctvnews.ca/politics/paralympian-trying-to-get-wheelchair-ramp-says-veterans-affairs-employee-offered-her-assisted-dying-1.6179325.

15. Jonathon Van Maren, "Canada's Killing Regime," *First Things*, October 18, 2022, https://www.firstthings.com/web-exclusives/2022/10/canadas-killing-regime.

16. Ibid.

17. Zahraa Hmood, "'Hunger Games Style Social Darwinism': Why Disability Advocates Are Worried About New Assisted Suicide Laws," *Niagara This Week*, September 19, 2022, https://www.thestar.com/local-st-catharines/life/2022/09/19/hunger-games-style-social-darwinism-why-disability-advocates-are-worried-about-new-assisted-suicide-laws.html.

18. Benjamin Lopez Steven, "Number of Assisted Deaths Jumped More Than 30 Per Cent in 2022, Report Says," CBC, October 27, 2023, https://www.cbc.ca/news/politics/maid-canada-report-2022-1.7009704.

19. Mona Gupta, "Canadians with Mental Disorders Shouldn't Be Excluded from Requesting MAID," *Maclean's*, May 4, 2023, https://macleans.ca/society/health/medical-assistance-in-dying/.

20. Ibid.

21. Poll conducted by Research Co. on Medical Assistance in Dying in Canada, Research Co., https://researchco.ca/wp-content/uploads/2023/05/Tables_MAiD_CAN_05May2023.pdf.

22. Reuters in The Hague, "Netherlands to Broaden Euthanasia Rules to Cover Children of All Ages," *Guardian*, April 14, 2023, https://www.theguardian.com/society/2023/apr/14/netherlands-to-broaden-euthanasia-rules-to-cover-children-of-all-ages.

23. Anna Lewis, "A Victim of Abuse Was Allowed to Choose Euthanasia," *Cosmopolitan*, May 11, 2016, https://www.cosmopolitan.com/uk/reports/news/a43244/sexual-abuse-victim-chose-euthanasia/.

24. "Should Anorexia Ever Be Called 'Terminal'?" *Washington Post*, November 1, 2023, https://www.washingtonpost.com/style/of-interest/2023/11/01/anorexia-suicide-controversy-jennifer-gaudiani/.

25. Patrick Reilly, "Physically Healthy Dutch Woman, 28, Decides to Be Euthanized Due to Crippling Depression," *New York Post*, April 2, 2024, https://nypost.com/2024/04/02/world-news/28-year-old-woman-decides-to-be-euthanized-due-to-mental-health-issues/.

26. Maria Cheng, "Some Dutch People Seeking Euthanasia Cite Autism or Intellectual Disabilities, Researchers Say," Associated Press, June 28, 2023, https://apnews.com/article/euthanasia-autism-intellectual-disabilities-netherlands-b5c4906d0305dd97e16da363575c03ae.

27. "Euthanasia: Dutch Court Expands Law on Dementia Cases," BBC, April 21, 2020, https://www.bbc.com/news/world-europe-52367644.

28. The Brussels Times Newsroom, "Nearly 4,000 People Opted for Euthanasia in Belgium in 2024," *Brussels Times*, March 19, 2025, https://www.brusselstimes.com/1493300/nearly-4000-people-opted-for-euthanasia-in-belgium-in-2024.

29. Kasper Raus, Bert Vanderhaegen, and Sigrid Sterckx, "Euthanasia in Belgium: Shortcomings of the Law and Its Application and of the Monitoring of Practice," *Journal of Medicine & Philosophy* 46, no. 1 (January 25, 2021): 80–107, https://doi.org/10.1093/jmp/jhaa031.

30. Harvard Medical School Center for Bioethics (@HMSbioethics) post on X, April 11, 2019, https://x.com/

HMSbioethics/status/1116357086022127616.

31. Michael Winter, "Deaf Belgian Twins Going Blind Choose to Be Euthanized," *USA Today*, January 14, 2013, https://www.usatoday.com/story/news/world/2013/01/14/deaf-belgian-twins-going-blind-euthanized/1834199/.

32. At the time of this writing, the UK is very close to taking a big vote on this issue (perhaps in April 2025), but a final vote is not likely until the end of 2025 or early 2026. The issue is also unclear but under discussion in Ireland, where public opinion remains mixed on the issue.

33. Danielle de Wolfe, "British Riding Start Caroline March Dies Aged 31 in Assisted Suicide After Career-Ending Spinal Cord Injury," LBC, March 25, 2024, https://www.lbc.co.uk/news/british-riding-star-caroline-march-dies-aged-31-in-assisted-suicide-after-career/.

34. Sasha Issenberg, "Hal Malchow Is Going to Die on Thursday. He Has One Last Message for Democrats," *Politico*, March 16, 2024, https://www.politico.com/news/magazine/2024/03/16/hal-malchow-scheduled-death-democrats-00147362.

35. Elizabeth Gilbert, "Americans More Than Ever Have No Friends. Here Are 5 Steps to Make More Friends," *Big Think*, April 15, 2023, https://bigthink.com/neuropsych/americans-no-friends/.

36. Andrew Van Dam, "The Political and Demographic Divides In Kitchen-Tool Ownership, and More!" *Washington Post*, December 1, 2023, https://www.washingtonpost.com/business/2023/12/01/most-common-kitchen-tools/.

37. Charles C. Camosy, "What's Behind the Nursing Home Horror," *New York Times*, May 17, 2020, https://www.nytimes.com/2020/05/17/opinion/nursing-home-coronavirus.html.

38. Gilbert, "No Friends."

39. Charles Camosy, "Who Gets to Decide if Charlie Gard's Life Is Worth Living? It Shouldn't Be His Doctors," *Washington Post*, July 13, 2017, https://www.washingtonpost.com/news/posteverything/wp/2017/07/13/who-gets-to-decide-if-charlie-gards-life-is-worth-living-it-shouldnt-be-his-doctors/.

40. John Wyatt, "End-of-Life Decisions, Quality of Life and the Newborn," *Acta Paediatrica* 96, no. 6 (May 24, 2007): 790–91, https://doi.org/10.1111/j.1651-2227.2007.00349.x.

41. Carlo V. Bellieni and Giuseppe Buonocore, "Flaws in the Assessment of the Best Interests of the Newborn," *Acta Paediatrica* 98, no. 4 (March 6, 2009): 613–17, https://doi.org/10.1111/j.1651-2227.2008.01185.x.

42. Charles Camosy, "On Not Dying Like a Physician," *Catholic Moral Theology*, December 13, 2011, https://catholicmoraltheology.com/on-not-dying-like-a-physcian/.

43. L. S. Dugdale, *The Lost Art of Dying: Reviving Forgotten Wisdom* (HarperOne, 2020), 71ff., Kindle.

44. AARP, *2018 Home and Community Preferences Survey: A National Survey of Adults Age 18-Plus*, August 2018, https://www.aarp.org/content/dam/aarp/research/surveys_statistics/liv-com/2018/home-community-preferences-survey.doi.10.26419-2Fres.00231.001.pdf.

45. Boone Ashworth, "Welcome to the Valley of the Creepy AI Dolls," *Wired*, March 9, 2024, https://www.wired.com/story/ai-dolls-for-older-adults/.

46. Jane Merrick, "Thousands of Disabled People Died After 'Covid Treatment Withheld', Inquiry to Probe," *The I Paper*, March 22, 2024, https://inews.co.uk/news/politics/thousands-of-disabled-people-died-after-covid-treatment-withheld-inquiry-to-probe-2970333.

47. "Phony Diagnoses Hide High Rates of Drugging at Nursing Homes," *New York Times*, September 12, 2021, https://www.nytimes.com/2021/09/11/health/nursing-homes-schizophrenia-antipsychotics.html.

48. Rachel Roberts, "Doctor Who Asked Dementia Patient's Family to Hold Her Down While She Gave Lethal Injection Cleared," *Independent*, February 5, 2017, https://www.the-independent.com/news/world/europe/doctor-netherlands-lethal-injection-dementia-euthanasia-a7564061.html.

49. Francis (@Pontifex), post on X, June 15, 2024, https://x.com/Pontifex/status/1801940215940227518.

50. Nicholas Goldberg, "California's Aid-in-Dying Law Is Working. Let's Expand It to Alzheimer's Patients," *Los Angeles Times*, July 15, 2020, https://www.latimes.com/opinion/story/2020-07-15/california-aid-in-dying-law-assisted-suicide-alzheimers-dementia.

51. Rachel Bluth, "For Terminal Patients, Dying in California May Get Easier," *Politico*, April 1, 2024, https://www.politico.com/news/2024/04/01/california-assisted-suicide-00149833.

52. Michael D. Connelly, *The Journey's End: An Investigation of Death and Dying in Modern America* (Rowman & Littlefield Publishers, 2023).

53. Adriana Diaz, "Immortality Is Attainable by 2030: Google Scientist," *New York Post*, March 29, 2023, https://nypost.com/2023/03/29/immortality-is-attainable-by-2030-google-scientist/.

54. Dugdale, *The Lost Art of Dying*, 101–2.

55. Leah Libresco Sargeant, "An Idol of Autonomy," *Dispatch*, January 13, 2025, https://thedispatch.com/article/an-idol-of-autonomy/.

Chapter Two: The Example of Christ

1. Allen Verhey, *The Christian Art of Dying: Learning from Jesus* (Wm B. Eerdmans, 2011).

2. *The Catholic Study Bible*, 3rd ed., ed. Donald Senior, John Collins, and Mary Ann Getty (Oxford University Press, 2016).

3. Much of what follows comes from Charles Camosy, *Losing Our Dignity: How Secularized Medicine Is Undermining Fundamental Human Equality* (New City Press, 2021).

4. Yolonda Wilson, "Why the Case of Jahi McMath Is Important for Understanding the Role of Race for Black Patients," *The Conversation*, July 12, 2018, https://theconversation.com/why-the-case-of-jahi-mcmath-is-important-for-understanding-the-role-of-race-for-black-patients-99353. For a deeper dive into this shameful history, readers may want to consult Harriet A. Washington, *Medical Apartheid: The Dark History of Medical Experimentation on Black Americans from Colonial Times to the Present* (Harlem Moon, 2001) and Rebecca Skloot, *The Immortal Life of Henrietta Lacks* (Broadway Books, 2011).

5. Todd L. Savitt, "The Use of Blacks for Medical Experimentation and Demonstration in the Old South," *Journal of Southern History* 48, no. 3 (August 1982): 331–48.

6. Pew Research Center, "Views on End-of-Life Medical Treatments: Growing Minority of Americans Say Doctors Should Do Everything Possible to Keep Patients Alive," Pew Forum, last updated November 21, 2013, https://www.pewforum.org/2013/11/21/views-on-end-of-life-medical-treatments/.

7. Sarah Varney, "Toward Hospice Care," *New York Times*, August 21, 2015, https://www.nytimes.com/2015/08/25/health/a-racial-gap-in-attitudes-toward-hospice-care.html.

8. Terri Laws, "How Race Matters in the Physician-Assisted Suicide Debate," *ARC*, September 3, 2019, https://arcmag.org/how-race-matters-in-the-physician-assisted-suicide-debate/.

9. Elissa Kozlov, et al., "Aggregating 23 Years of Data on Medical Eid in Dying in the United States," *Journal of American Geriatrics Society* 70, no. 10 (June 16, 2022): 3040–44, https://doi.org/10.1111/jgs.17925.

10. Oregon Health Authority, "Oregon Death with Dignity Act 2023 Data Summary," March 20, 2024, https://www.oregon.gov/oha/PH/PROVIDERPARTNERRESOURCES/EVALUATIONRESEARCH/DEATHWITHDIGNITYACT/Documents/year26.pdf.

Chapter Three: Three Catholic Saints on Dying Well

1. Francis, *Patris Corde*, December 8, 2020, Vatican.va.

2. *Patris Corde*, par. 4.

3. John C. Cavadini, "The Fatherly Heart of Saint Joseph," *Church Life Journal*, January 26, 2021, https://churchlifejournal.nd.edu/articles/the-fatherly-heart-of-saint-joseph/.

4. Oblates of St. Joseph, "For a Happy Death," https://osjusa.org/prayers/for-a-happy-death/.

5. "St. Teresa of Avila Passing," Catholic Contemplative Life, August 11, 2022, https://humanityfaithhopecharity.com/2022/08/11

/st-teresa-of-avila-passing/.

6. Slavomír Gálik, Sabína Gáliková Tolnaiová, and Arkadiusz Modrzejewski, "Mystical Death in the Spirituality of Saint Teresa of Ávila," *Sophia* 59 (2020): 593–612, https://doi.org/10.1007/s11841-020-00763-y.

7. Gálik, Tolnaiová, and Modrzejewski, "Mystical Death."

8. Charles C. Camosy, "What the Far-Left Might Learn from Cardinal Bellarmine's View of Science," Religion News Service, August 14, 2020, https://religionnews.com/2020/08/14/what-the-far-left-might-learn-from-cardinal-bellarmines-view-of-science/.

9. Robert Bellarmine, *The Art of Dying Well*, trans. Rev. John Dalton (Richardson and Son, [1847?]).

10. Ibid., chap. 4.

11. Ibid.

12. Ibid., chap. 9.

13. Ibid.

14. Ibid., chap. 5.

Chapter Four: The Example of Catholic Monks and Friars

1. Daniel P. Horan, "Embracing Sister Death: The Fraternal Worldview of Francis of Assisi as a Source of Christian Eschatological Hope," *The Other Journal*, no. 14, https://theotherjournal.com/2009/01/embracing-sister-death-the-fraternal-worldview-of-francis-of-assisi-as-a-source-for-christian-eschatological-hope/.

2. Augustine Thompson, *Francis of Assisi: A New Biography* (Cornell University Press, 2012), 84.

3. Francis of Assisi, early documents, accessed at Franciscan Tradition, https://digitalcollections.franciscantradition.org/document/bx4700-f6f722-1999/francis_of_assisi_early_documents_-_the_saint/1999-00-00.

4. Mary Petrosky, *Dying, as a Franciscan: Approaching Our Transitus to Eternal Life, Accompanying Others on the Way to Theirs* (Franciscan

Institute Publications, 2011), 34–35.

5. David Torkington, "St Francis of Assisi — Welcome Sister Death," *Catholic Stand*, October 4, 2018, https://catholicstand.com/st-francis-of-assisi-welcome-sister-death/.

6. Donald F. Duclow, "Ars Moriendi," *Encyclopedia of Death and Dying*, http://www.deathreference.com/A-Bi/Ars-Moriendi.html.

7. Verhey, *The Christian Art of Dying*, 82.

8. Stephen E. Doran, M.D., *To Die Well: A Catholic Neurosurgeon's Guide to the End of Life* (Ignatius Press, 2023), 103.

9. Dugdale, *The Lost Art of Dying*, 36.

10. Nicolas Diat, *A Time to Die: Monks on the Threshold of Eternal Life* (Ignatius Press, 2019).

11. Ibid.
12. Ibid.
13. Ibid.
14. Ibid.
15. Ibid.
16. Ibid.
17. Ibid.
18. Ibid.
19. Ibid.
20. Ibid.

Chapter Five: Care Homes and Hospices Today

1. Rachel Roubein, "Will the Nursing Home of the Future Be an Actual Home?" *Politico*, April 30, 2021, https://www.politico.com/news/agenda/2021/04/30/nursing-home-future-483460.

2. William E. Phipps, "The Origin of Hospices/Hospitals," *Death Studies* 12, no. 2 (1988): 91–99, Taylor & Francis Online, https://www.tandfonline.com/doi/abs/10.1080/07481188808252226.

3. "History of Hospice," Hospice Society of Camrose and District, https://www.camrosehospice.org/history-of-hospice.

4. Saul Ebema, "What Are the Unique Origins of Hospice?"

Hospice Chaplaincy, January 3, 2018, https://hospicechaplaincy.com/2018/01/03/hospice-origins/.

5. "About Santa Teresita," Santa Teresita, https://www.santa-teresita.org/about/.

6. Ibid.

7. These and all the following details come from email correspondence with the Carmelite Sisters.

8. Little Sisters of the Poor, "Who We Are," https://www.littlesistersofthepoor.org/our-vocation/.

9. Constance Veit, "Humble Service and Merciful Love to America," *Boston Pilot*, July 11, 2018, https://thebostonpilot.com/opinion/article.asp?ID=182774.

10. Ibid.

11. Little Sisters of the Poor, "Who We Are."

12. These materials are from Sister Constance via email.

13. "Reframing End-of-Life Care During COVID," January 27, 2021, posted by Catholic Information Center, YouTube, https://www.youtube.com/watch?v=-jPRLmdRcbI&t=463s.

14. Little Sisters of the Poor, "Our Vocation," https://littlesistersofthepoor.org/our-vocation/.

15. Constance Veit, "The Best Is Yet to Come," *Boston Pilot*, September 21, 2022, https://thebostonpilot.com/opinion/article.asp?ID=193251.

16. The Editors, "Hospice Providers Must Be Better Regulated," *Scientific American*, February 1, 2024, https://www.scientificamerican.com/article/hospice-providers-must-be-better-regulated/.

17. Bob Tedeschi, "Against a History of Medical Mistreatment, African-Americans Are Distrustful of Hospice Care," *STAT*, April 5, 2017, https://www.statnews.com/2017/04/05/hospice-care-african-americans/.

18. Leah Libresco Sargeant, "The Gift of Palliative Care," *Plough*, February 28, 2023, https://www.plough.com/en/topics/life/work/the-gift-of-palliative-care.

19. "Medical Pioneer and Compassionate Healer, Dr. Michael Brescia," Calvary Hospital, April 21, 2023, https://www.calvaryhospital.org/medical-pioneer-and-compassionate-healer-dr-michael-brescia/.

20. "The Vestibule of Heaven," *Imprint* (Winter 2017), posted at Sisters of Life, https://sistersoflife.org/2019/08/27/hello-world-3-3-2-2/.

21. The remaining material in this section comes from email correspondence with Sister Agnus Dei of the Sisters of Life, who shared notes from her exchanges with Dr. Brescia.

Chapter Six: Resisting Physician-Assisted Killing as Individuals

1. Doran, *To Die Well*, chap. 11.

2. Mike Schmitz, "The Key to a Happy Death," Ascension Presents, https://media.ascensionpress.com/video/the-key-to-a-happy-death/.

3. Verhey, *The Christian Art of Dying*, 312.

4. Ibid.

5. Charles C. Camosy, "New Book Urges Reflections on 'Last Things' During Advent," *Crux*, November 20, 2021, https://cruxnow.com/interviews/2021/11/new-book-urges-reflections-on-last-things-during-advent.

6. Theresa Aletheia Noble, *Memento Mori: An Advent Companion on the Last Things* (Pauline Books & Media, 2021).

7. Theresa Aletheia Noble, FSP, *Memento Mori Perpetual Desk Calendar* (Pauline Books & Media, 2021).

8. Marianna Orlandi, "To Die Well, We Must Live Well — And for Others," *Public Discourse*, September 24, 2024, https://www.thepublicdiscourse.com/2024/09/95962.

9. Gilbert Meilaender, "I Want to Burden My Loved Ones," *First Things*, March 1, 2010, https://www.firstthings.com/article/2010/03/i-want-to-burden-my-loved-ones.

10. Charles C. Camosy, "Honoring the Elderly," *First Things*, July 26, 2020, https://www.firstthings.com/web-exclusives/2020/07/honoring-the-elderly/.

Chapter Seven: Resisting Physician-Assisted Killing as Families

1. Ari Schulman (@AriSchulman), post on X, November 22, 2024, https://x.com/AriSchulman/status/1860150918093885835.
2. Dugdale, *The Lost Art of Dying*, 71–72.
3. John Paul II, *Laborem Exercens*, Vatican.va, 19, bold emphasis added.
4. Vincenzo Paglia and Renzo Pegoraro, "Old Age: Our Future," February 2, 2021, Vatican.va, https://www.vatican.va/roman_curia/pontifical_academies/acdlife/documents/rc_pont-acd_life_doc_20210202_vecchiaia-nostrofuturo_en.html.
5. John Soriano, "What We Lost," *First Things*, January 31, 2022, https://www.firstthings.com/web-exclusives/2022/01/what-we-lost.
6. Noreen Madden McInnes, *Keep at It Riley! Accompanying My Father through Death into Life* (New City Press, 2022), chap. 8.
7. Ibid., chap. 9.
8. Ibid., chap. XX.
9. Charlie Camosy, "'From Death into Life' — Loving a Sick or Dying Parent," *The Pillar*, April 8, 2022, https://www.pillarcatholic.com/p/from-death-into-life-loving-a-sick.

Chapter Eight: Resisting Physician-Assisted Killing as Communities and Institutions

1. Paglia and Pegoraro, "Old Age: Our Future."
2. 2024 Republican Party Platform, American Presidency Project, July 8, 2024, https://www.presidency.ucsb.edu/documents/2024-republican-party-platform.
3. Charles C. Camosy, "Honoring the Elderly," *First Things*, July 26, 2020, https://www.firstthings.com/web-exclusives/2020/07/honoring-the-elderly.
4. "Homelessness and Housing: A Human Tragedy, a Moral Challenge," USCCB, March 24, 1988, paras. 5–6, https://www.usccb.org/resources/homelessness-and-housing-human-tragedy-moral-challenge/.

5. "Catholic Hospitals Comprise One Quarter of the World's Healthcare, Council Reports," Catholic News Agency, February 10, 2010, https://www.catholicnewsagency.com/news/18624/catholic-hospitals-comprise-one-quarter-of-worlds-healthcare-council-reports.

6. "U.S. Catholic Health Care," 2019 mini profile, Catholic Health Association of the United States, https://www.chausa.org/docs/default-source/default-document-library/cha_2019_miniprofile.pdf.

7. Anne Maria Barry-Jester and Amelia Thomson-DeVeaux, "How Catholic Bishops Are Shaping Health Care in Rural America," FiveThirtyEight (ABC News), July 25, 2018, https://fivethirtyeight.com/features/how-catholic-bishops-are-shaping-health-care-in-rural-america/.

8. Connelly, *The Journey's End*, chap. 14.

9. Paglia and Pegoraro, "Old Age: Our Future."

10. It is worth noting that there is at least some hope that we can bend the trends in a different direction, especially if it is true that many forms of dementia are caused by metabolic disease. See Thuy Trang Nguyen, Qui Thanh Hoai Ta, Thi Kim Oanh Nguyen, and Vo Van Giau, "Type 3 Diabetes and Its Role Implications in Alzheimer's Disease," *Int. J. Mol. Sci.* 21, no. 9 (April 30, 2020), https://www.mdpi.com/1422-0067/21/9/3165. It is also possible that trends may accelerate in the other direction.

11. George G. Glenner Alzheimer's Family Centers, Inc., "Who We Are," https://glenner.org/#our-mission.

12. George G. Glenner Alzheimer's Family Centers, Inc., "What We Do," https://glenner.org/services/adult-day-care/.

13. Amanda Kolson Hurley, "Time-Travel Therapy," *Atlantic*, January/February 2017, https://www.theatlantic.com/magazine/archive/2017/01/time-travel-therapy/508787/.

14. Charles Camosy, "We Need a St. Frances Cabrini to Address Our Dementia Crisis," *Angelus*, April 25, 2024, https://angelusnews.com/voices/california-dementia-cabrini/.

15. Dan Stockman, "Congregations Seek Ways to Turn Empty

Convents into New Ministries," *National Catholic Reporter*, March 18, 2024, https://www.ncronline.org/congregations-seek-ways-turn-empty-convents-new-ministries. Notre Dame also has a program that is trying to help streamline this kind of process: See the Fitzgerald Institute for Real Estate Church Properties Initiative, https://churchproperties.nd.edu.

16. Kyra Miles, "In Minneapolis, Caregivers Connect Kids and Seniors — and Everyone Benefits," MPR News, September 16, 2024, https://www.mprnews.org/story/2024/09/16/in-minneapolis-caregivers-connect-kids-with-seniors-and-everyone-benefits.

17. Ibid.

18. The following paragraph restates in different words a central point previously argued in the conclusion of Charles C. Camosy, *Losing Our Dignity* (New City Press, 2021).

About the Author

Charlie Camosy teaches moral theology and bioethics at The Catholic University of America. He served formerly as Professor of Medical Humanities at the Creighton University School of Medicine and holds the Monsignor Curran Fellowship in Moral Theology at St. Joseph Seminary in New York. Before that, he spent fourteen years in Fordham University's theology department, where he taught since finishing his PhD in moral theology at Notre Dame in 2008. Among other places, his articles have appeared in the American Journal of Bioethics, Journal of Medicine and Philosophy, Journal of the Catholic Health Association, New York Times, Washington Post, New York Daily News and America magazine. He has monthly columns with Religion News Service and does regular Q&As for OSV News. He is the author of nine books. Beyond the Abortion Wars (Eerdmans), was a 2015 award-winner with the Catholic Media Association, and Resisting Throwaway Culture (New City) was named 2020 "Resource of the Year" by the Catholic Publishers Association. He is also the founding editor of a book series with New City Press called The Magenta Project. In addition to receiving the 2018 St. Jerome Award for scholarly excellence from the Catholic Library Association and the 2024 Smith Award from the University Faculty for Life, Charlie is a proud knight of the St. Peter Claver Society. He and his wife, Paulyn, have four children, three of whom they adopted from a Filipino orphanage in June of 2016.